Kansas
CURIOSITIES

Help Us Keep This Guide Up to Date

Every effort has been made by the author and editors to make this guide as accurate and useful as possible. However, many things can change after a guide is published—establishments close, phone numbers change, hiking trails are rerouted, facilities come under new management, etc.

We would love to hear from you concerning your experiences with this guide and how you feel it could be made better and be kept up to date. While we may not be able to respond to all comments and suggestions, we'll take them to heart and we'll also make certain to share them with the author. Please send your comments and suggestions to the following address:

Globe Pequot Press
Reader Response/Editorial Department
P.O. Box 480
Guilford, CT 06437

Or you may e-mail us at:
editorial@GlobePequot.com

Thanks for your input, and happy travels!

Curiosities Series

Kansas
CURIOSITIES

Quirky characters,
roadside oddities &
other offbeat stuff

Third Edition

Pam Grout

Guilford, Connecticut

The prices, rates, and hours listed in this guidebook were con-
firmed at press time. We recommend, however, that you call
establishments to obtain current information before traveling.

Copyright © 2010 by Morris Book Publishing, LLC

Photos by Pam Grout unless otherwise noted.
Maps by Sue Murray © Morris Book Publishing, LLC
Text design: Bret Kerr
Layout artist: Casey Shain
Project editor: John Burbidge

Library of Congress Cataloging-in-Publication data is available on file.

ISBN 978-0-7627-5863-0
ISSN 1932-7331

Printed in the United States of America

10 9 8 7 6 5 4 3 2

For my dad, a reformed Texan, who didn't balk when the call came to preach in Kansas, and for my mom, a Michigander who, to this day, will travel anywhere.

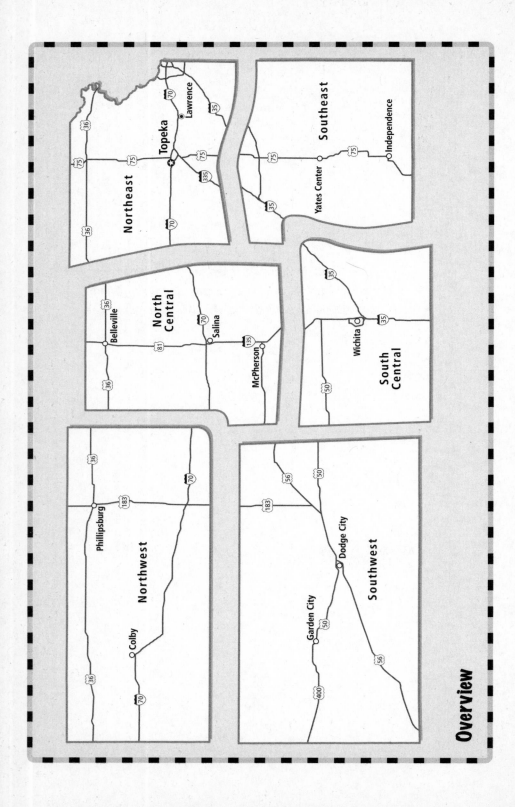

Overview

contents

* *

acknowledgments

★ ★

*B*ig hugs to all the folks in Kansas who happily opened their arms and hearts in helping me research this book.

Special thanks to Beverly Hurley; Marci Penner (I still think you should be Explorer #1); Maria Butler, who made my year by picking the second edition of this book as the "Read Across Lawrence" selection in 2008; and all the brave and fearless Kansas Explorers. Also thanks to Meredith Davis, John Burbidge and the other folks at Globe Pequot Press who have helped me avoid having to get a real job.

★ ★

Remember that Milton Bradley game Operation, where you used tweezers to surgically remove such plastic body parts as Water on the Knee (a tiny bucket) and Bread Basket (a tiny piece of bread with one bite gnawed out)? It was a favorite in the Grout household, which is saying a lot since we Grouts are big game players from way back. I'm sure whatever relatives we might have had on the Mayflower spent most of the voyage on the poop deck playing Monopoly.

My sister Becki and I devoted many a summer afternoon to extricating itty-bitty plastic ailments from poor Cavity Sam's decrepit body. In all our years of playing Operation, neither of us could successfully remove the petite plastic pencil known as Writer's Cramp without grazing the tweezers on the metal ridge. At the start of every new contest, we'd vow, much like Mel Fisher in his search for the Atocha, "This is the day we'll get that pencil." But every single time, Sam's battery-powered red nose would light up, ending our quest. We eventually concluded it was humanly impossible.

Which is pretty much how I feel about the third edition of this book. Figuring out which old fascinating, amazing things to amputate to make way for new fascinating, amazing things was humanly impossible. I had to perform surgery on a book I already liked a heck of an awful lot.

To offset the emotional turmoil of saying goodbye to such old friends as Franny's dollar lunches and Ruby Meyers's full-size papier-mâché three-ring circus, I got to learn about a slew of new curiosities. I was privileged to meet Harley, the motorcycle-riding yellow lab, and Bill Woods, an eighty-year-old former aerospace engineer who was putting the finishing touches on a team of twenty-four oxen that he made from still-full Boost bottles (it's a protein energy drink) that his son insisted on sending. He used them as an art medium instead.

So, yes, Cavity Sam's nose keeps lighting up. But it shines on the ever-new, ever-exciting, ever-expanding oddities of Kansas.

J wasn't lucky enough to be born in Kansas. But when I was four, my father, a freshly scrubbed ministerial student from Kentucky's Asbury College, landed his first preaching assignment in Canton, Kansas, home of a pair of hot and cold water towers. Other than my ski bum gypsy period and a few stints overseas, I've lived in Kansas ever since.

Dad's days off were Monday through Saturday (he had to preach, of course, on Sunday), so we spent a lot of time driving the state in our red 1964 Rambler station wagon. I figured every kid got to tramp around five acres of giant mushroom rocks, pray with Mennonites, and eat quarter-size hamburgers at Cozy Inn. I had no idea how lucky I was.

As I grew older, I started hearing nasty rumors. I learned that some people in this country thought Kansas was flat (they obviously hadn't been to the lookout near White Cloud, where you can see four states) and boring. *Spy* magazine, in fact, had the audacity to call Kansas the "most boringest state in the Union."

Obviously, whoever wrote that, besides being functionally illiterate, had never been here. I mean, c'mon, Kansas has more statues of liberty than New York.

Twenty-six, in fact, that were erected between 1949 and 1951 by Boy Scout troops around the state that were able to raise $350, the price at that time for an 8-foot lady of liberty.

For a while though, I have to admit, I bought into it. I was an impressionable teenager. I made plans to "go west, young woman." I wanted to be king of the hill, top of the heap, New York, New York.

And then I figured it out.

Kansans don't need or want the glory. Why waste our time defending ourselves or disputing jealous detractors? Like Archie Bunker, those prejudiced busybodies have already made up their minds. Most of them have never been here anyway, and those who have probably never bothered to get off I-70 (except maybe to take a pee at Stuckey's).

As far as we're concerned, people can believe the rumors. We're too busy and far too happy and prosperous here in Kansas to worry about other people's misinformation. If we supported a tourism budget like

★ ★

Nevada or California, if people really knew all there was to see and do here, we might have crowded freeways and drive-by shootings like Los Angeles. The way we figure it, we don't need spin doctors touting our state. We already have everything we need.

One summer during college, I took a job with the Kansas Department of Economic Development. At that time, Kansas

Perchance the only state with two towns with hot and cold water towers?

was the only state that didn't have an official tourism department. My job, along with three other journalism interns, was to drive around the state in a big RV and promote Kansas, see if we couldn't lure people into sticking around a day or two longer.

The governor loaded us down with brochures, gave us a gasoline credit card, and sent us off to "go forth and be prosperous." To this day, I regard it as one of the best jobs I've ever had. Not only was I paid $700 a month, a veritable fortune for a college kid in those days (my friends were barmaids earning minimum wage), but I got to stay in hotels with maid service and clean sheets and visit all of Kansas's hot spots. If there was a festival on the eastern side of the state (the two girls traveled the east while the two boys took the west), we were there, setting up our folding table, passing out our brochures, and chatting up cute boys.

We went to swap meets and tractor pulls, barbecue cook-offs and fishing tournaments. We even, if I'm not mistaken, went to Skunk Run Days in Ottawa.

There was the John Brown Jamboree in Osawatomie, the intertribal powwow in Council Grove, and Chingawassa Days in Marion.

I never had it so good. In fact, the only drawback at all was the disappointment on some rock'n'roll fans' faces when they stopped by our motor home—which had the word *Kansas* splashed across it in 3-foot-high letters—and discovered we weren't the rock group Kansas after all. Considering that the group's hits, "Dust in the Wind" and "Carry on, Wayward Son," were leading the Top 40, their dismay was not surprising.

Unfortunately, a couple of weeks before our internship was scheduled to end, I flipped a dead wasp at Patty, my fellow explorer, who drove the brand-new RV with the painted letters into a ditch. Totaled it. We had to spend the last two weeks of our assignment in Topeka at a Holiday Inn near the state office building, where we reported each day to write assessments of our travels. "Where," the bigwigs wanted to know, "would you recommend a permanent tourism booth?" I don't remember what we wrote, but I do remember those stuffy offices weren't half as much fun as traveling the back roads of Kansas.

In California, the beauty is obvious. Any idiot can see it. Kansas, I'm proud to say, is every bit as beautiful, it's just more subtle. You have to be sharp. Here in Kansas we don't have mountains to ski down (well, we do have one ski slope, Mount Bleu, outside Lawrence) or waves to surf, so we have to find our own way. We've had to use our initiative, make our own fun, create our own art. And that is exactly why you find startling inventions like the helicopter and the Slurpee coming out of Kansas. That's why we have more folk artists per capita than anywhere in the world. It's why Inez Marshall carved full-size Abraham Lincolns and Harley-Davidsons out of limestone, why Leroy Wilson painted his basement over and over again for twelve years.

So let other people make fun of Kansas. What do we care if they

★ ★

believe our state is dull and backward? That mistaken identity just leaves more room for us.

Most of us, in fact, choose to play up our less than stellar reputation. When Howard Stern's producer called a couple of years ago to set up an interview with the famous New York shock jock about a book I wrote, I figured I might as well play into his hick jokes. Because I knew our radio interview (with me on the phone in Kansas, him in his New York studio) was being videotaped for his show on E!, I went out and bought a pair of overalls. I even considered putting a blade of hay in my mouth.

As I said, we like to have fun here in Kansas.

Today, as an adult, I write a travel column called "Now, Where Was I?" Frequently I'm called upon to leave the borders of my home state, to write about places like Australia or Portugal or Bermuda. With this book, I finally got to stay home for a change. It is with great delight that I took on this assignment, that I was able to write this book with not just a few, but more than 200 listings about my favorite state.

Good old Dorothy was right, there's no place like Kansas. I think as you read the pages that follow, you'll come to agree.

More Powerful than a Locomotive, More Liberal than California

Before we go any further, I've got some bubbles to burst, a couple myths that need dispelling.

About the tornadoes, I can't dismiss the fact that we've had a few over the years. In fact, there used to be a town called Irving, up in northeastern Kansas, that was hit by two tornadoes in one day, something weather forecasters claim is a statistical impossibility.

On May 30, 1879, a little after 4 p.m., the first tornado hit, killing six at the Gale residence (none, as far as I know, was named Dorothy), breaking every bone in the bodies of tethered livestock, and picking up a wagon carrying a thousand board feet of lumber, which was never seen again. Hardly had the folks of Irving recovered from the first shock

Did somebody say something about flat?
CHARLIE REIDEL

when the second tornado blew in from a different direction, flattening what was left.

In another incident, in what used to be Codell in Reno County, a twister struck on May 20, 1916, May 20, 1917, and May 20, 1918. May 20, 1919, I'm happy to report, was a beautiful spring day.

But despite these anomalies, the fact remains that Kansas is not even remotely close to being the state with the most tornadoes per year. In fact, it's fourth, behind Texas, Oklahoma, and Florida. And if you're keeping tabs on killer tornadoes, it doesn't even make the top ten.

And then there's the issue of being backward. All I can say is, Kansas women have been voting, holding office, and passing bills for almost two centuries. In 1888 an all-woman town council led by a female mayor was elected in Oskaloosa. This, I hasten to point out, was thirty-two years before women in the rest of the country could even vote. And Oskaloosa's wasn't the first female mayor. Argonia elected Susanna Salter a year earlier.

Kansas was also the first state to ratify the Fifteenth Amendment, giving blacks the right to vote. It was the first to advocate a forty-hour workweek, and the first to push for the 1906 pure food and drug laws.

When Kansas was first settled, it was a place of daring social experimentation. Whole communities were established on such progressive concepts as racial equality, vegetarianism, socialism, and open marriage. In the 1890s, an Irish promoter even convinced English dukes and lords to send their lazy sons to Kansas to train in the art of farming. Runnymede, one of dozens of communities started in Kansas, had a racetrack, a polo field, a steeplechase course, and an official purpose: to dispense agrarian knowledge to the frivolous rich. Hundreds of reform newspapers were published in Kansas, including *Lucifer the Light-Bringer,* a Valley Falls weekly vehement in its quest for equal marriage rights.

Some of the bold experiments failed. Other prospered and led the way in social, religious, and political freedoms for the entire nation.

As journalist William Allen White once said, "Things start in Kansas that finish in history."

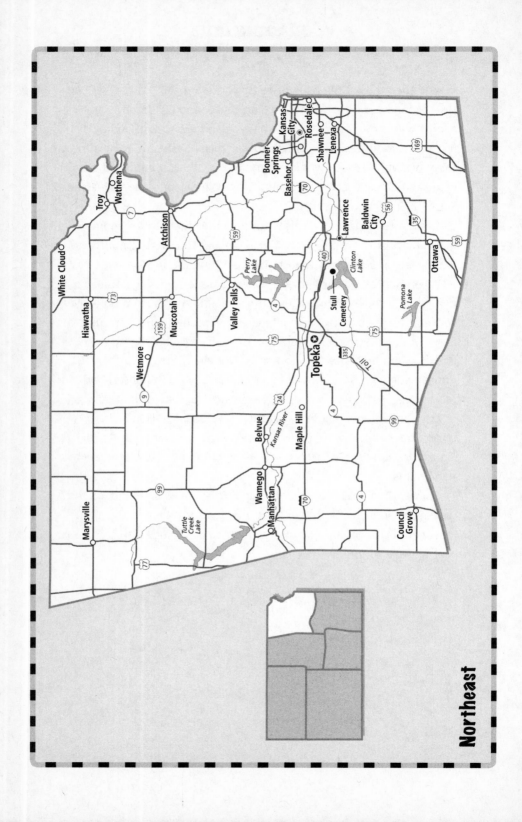

Northeast

1

Northeast

If it weren't *for the northeast corner, the state of Kansas would resemble a perfect rectangle, 400 miles long and 200 miles high. Luckily, that end of Kansas looks like a ravenous mastodon came along and gnawed off a big chunk. To my mind, that gives our asymmetrical state a little personality. A tad bit of geographic charisma.*

The northeast, of course, claims Kansas City, the state's eponymous and most well-known city, but truth be told, most of what people associate with Kansas City—the Chiefs, the jazz, the barbecue—is situated in the other Kansas City, the one a stone's throw across the river in that wannabe—Missouri.

The one with all the flair—Strawberry Hill and the Ag Hall of Fame— is on our side. Again, we Kansans are kinda busy to spend much time bragging about it.

The northeast also has lots of little towns with fascinating graveyards, motorcycles built out of pull tabs and bones (both chicken legs and cow mandibles), and architecture you won't find in any Frank Lloyd Wright museum. Or at least last we checked, the famous architect, wasn't setting old pickups in concrete.

★ ★

And They Said the Moon Had No Trees

Atchison

I've heard of some pretty crazy gardening techniques—mixing beer with apple juice and ammonia, using Juicy Fruit gum to ward off moles—but the International Forest of Friendship on the slopes of Lake Warnock outside of Atchison might just take the cake. Tree planters there sent a sycamore seed all the way to the moon and back before sticking it in the ground. The Moon Tree, as it's called, was planted from a seed that Command Pilot Stuart Roosa took with him on Apollo 14.

The forest was planted in 1976 when the Ninety-Nines, the international organization of women pilots, decided to uphold the wish of their first president, Amelia Earhart, who dreamed of world peace through flying. They sent out a plea to members the world over: "Send your native saplings to Amelia's hometown of Atchison."

The saplings, now more than thirty years old, grew into a forest. Joining the Moon Tree are trees from all fifty states and more than

To infinity and beyond!
MARY BETH HOWE-BERNHARDT

2

One giant sycamore for mankind.
MARY BETH HOWE-BERNHARDT

forty countries, a cherry tree from George Washington's Mount Vernon estate, and a redbud from President Eisenhower's home. In addition to a bronze statue of Amelia, there's a walkway called Memory Lane that has more than 700 plaques commemorating aviation and notable pilots the world over.

On the third weekend of June, the Ninety-Nines add three or four new names and plaques. The forest is located a mile south of the junction of US 59 and US 73. Call (913) 367-1419 or check out www.ninety-nines.org for more info.

★ ★

President du Jour
Atchison

Unlike most states, Kansas has two presidential libraries. It also has a presidential loser's library (the Dole Institute in Lawrence, which even has clips of Bob Dole's infamous Viagra commercial) and a gallery of Oval Office wannabes (The Gallery of Also-Rans in Norton, see Northwest chapter).

The older of our two presidential libraries, the Eisenhower Museum and Library in Abilene, is pretty well-known. It's one of ten presidential libraries administered by the National Archives and Records Administration. It gets thousands of tourists each year.

Our other presidential library, the one that honors our twelfth president (no, not Zachary Taylor, he was the thirteenth and hailed from Virginia) is little more than a 35-square-foot kiosk inside the restored Santa Fe Depot that serves as the Atchison County History Museum. Only a few people see it each year.

I should probably explain. David Rice Atchison served as U.S. President for one short day, which could account for why he's usually left off the official list of former presidents. By a quirk of fate, Atchison assumed office when newly elected president Zachary Taylor, a religious man, refused to take the oath of office on a Sunday.

At midnight on Saturday, March 3, 1849, incumbent James Polk's term ended. Since March 4, when Taylor should have taken the oath, happened to fall on a Sunday, he put it off until Monday, March 5, so no one could accuse him of defiling the Sabbath for something as insignificant as a little oath of office.

Atchison, who was president pro tem of the Senate, was, of course, next in line for the job. During his twenty-four hours in office, he didn't declare war or appoint any of his cronies to office, but he did turn his "unofficial" presidency into a great story.

The Atchison County History Museum has taken its namesake's lead, turning its "world's smallest presidential library" into a great story as well. The kiosk that serves as the presidential library contains

★ ★

a picture of Atchison, who was born in Frogville, Kentucky; a Civil War pistol he once owned; the one biography written about him; and a copy of his Senate speeches.

To visit the world's smallest presidential library, go to the Atchison County History Museum, located at 200 South Tenth Street (913-367-6238; www.atchisonhistory.org).

Glad I Didn't Have to Dust Buckingham Palace
Baldwin City

A tiny 24-by-40-foot chapel in Baldwin City was singularly responsible for England's Great Sawdust Shortage of 1995. But that can happen when you're shipping 25,000 stones across the ocean. Ten thousand pounds of sawdust, Great Britain's entire supply, was stuffed into crates that held the 250 tons of rocks sent by ship, by truck, and by rail to Kansas.

Maybe I should start at the beginning.

In 1864, the Methodist congregation in Sproxton, England, a little town about 100 miles north of London, built a church. For six decades this spunky congregation had been meeting in homes of local parishioners, so having a real building was a big deal. All I can think is that they must have had an awful lot of bake sales. The church prospered (which undoubtedly meant more bake sales) for more than a century. But by 1988 the congregation had shrunk and the tiny chapel was forced to close. About the same time, Baker University in Baldwin City got a new dean. He hated to be pushy, but hey, how can a Methodist college not have a chapel on campus?

Up steps the husband of Clarice L. Osborne, a banker in nearby Olathe. He's looking for some way to honor his deceased wife, so he throws a cool million in the offering plate to bring the church with no congregation to the university with no church.

The Sproxton church was literally taken apart, and all 25,000 pieces were numbered, packed in crates (with five tons of sawdust), and sent to Baldwin. It was reassembled like Legos and dedicated by

Margaret Thatcher (her dad, Alfred Roberts, used to preach at the little church) on October 23, 1996.

To see this miracle of modern masonry, visit the Clarice L. Osborne Memorial Chapel on the campus of Baker University in Baldwin City. The chapel is open each day from 8 a.m. to 8 p.m. Call (785) 594-4553 for more info or go to www.bakeru.edu/baldwin/prospective-students/spiritual-life/osborne-chapel.

Tom Sawyer Would Be Proud
Basehor

Tom Sawyer—who raked in a kite, twelve marbles, six firecrackers, a tin soldier, and a cat with one eye for allowing his friends to white-wash Aunt Polly's fence—has nothing on Les and Michelle Meyer. The father-daughter owners of Holy-Field Vineyard & Winery have come up with a fall harvest scheme so clever that loyal customers literally fight over the chance to help them pick grapes.

Reservations (and you simply MUST secure reservations) for their picking Sundays, five late summer and fall Sunday mornings when the entire fifteen-acre vineyard is picked clean, fill up faster than you can say American and French hybrid varietals. If you wait until the fall to reserve your space, you will definitely be S.O.L.

But then Les and Michelle have been forced to be crafty. Running a winery in a state that didn't even allow liquor by the drink until 1987 is no small feat. In 2001, *Kiplinger's Personal Finance* magazine ran a two-page spread about Holy-Field, raving about its Chambourcin, declaring it the best of sixty-five nonviniferas they sampled. Needless to say, phones started ringing off the wall. All Michelle could do was grit her teeth and tell the potential customers that Kansas law prohibited her from shipping wine. If they wanted to get a bottle or a case, which many wanted to order, they'd either have to come and get it or send friends.

The Meyers have concocted many a scheme to lure customers to "come and get it." Besides the "sold-out" grape-picking weekends,

American Gothic without the pitchfork.
WAYNE RHODUS

★ ★

they offer jazz at the vineyard every May, June, and July and murder-mystery dinners with such clever titles as "It's a Wonderful Death," "When Irish Spies Are Dying," and "Gone with the Passing of the Wind." They also sell an incredible box of wine-filled chocolates.

The Meyers planted their first vines in 1986, primarily for personal enjoyment. As the volume increased and friends insisted, they officially launched Holy-Field Vineyard & Winery in 1994. For four years they kept their day jobs. Les was a successful hairdresser. Michelle ran the community blood bank. But then the awards started piling up. In 2005 alone, Holy-Field wines won thirty-one national and international awards.

Holy-Field Vineyard & Winery, including its wine production cellar, tasting room, and gift shop, is located at 18807 158th Street, just west of Basehor. Call (913) 724-9463 or visit them online at www.holyfieldwinery.com.

Art to Si(lo) For
Belvue

They might look like ordinary everyday silos to the average eye, but to a Kansan, those ubiquitous grain storage bins call to us for more. Make us your canvas, they practically scream. In Emporia, there's a silo that's a spitting image of a Coors beer can. Less than a mile away, there's a red and white Coca-Cola can.

The Western Resources Oregon Trail Nature Park near Belvue had higher aspirations. The 30-foot silo there has three giant depictions of early Kansas history. There's even a giant map of the Oregon Trail. Onaga artist Cindy Martin was commissioned by Western Resources, owners of the sixty-acre park, to paint the silo in 1995.

To reach the giant easel, visit Western Resources Oregon Trail Nature Park, a mile east of Belvue, just north of US 24. Phone (785) 456-2035.

Onaga artist Cindy Martin proves great art doesn't grow on trees.
MARY BETH HOWE-BERNHARDT

★ ★

Lost Your Marbles? Find Them at "The Moon"

Bonner Springs

Bruce Breslow has heard all the jokes. And he's happy to laugh because while everybody else is losing their marbles, he's busy making replacements. His Moon Marble Company is a one-of-a-kind general store with all kinds of marbles (ever seen marbles with busts of dead presidents inside?), as well as games and toys.

The most "marble-ous" collection in the Sunflower State.
JASON GIBBENS, COURTESY OF MOON MARBLE COMPANY

★ ★

If you call ahead, Breslow will show you his "marble field," two big circles painted on the green carpet, and teach you how to knuckle down.

Ask nicely, and he'll even demonstrate how marbles are made, a unique glassblowing technique that requires a blowtorch, special glasses, and a kiln where the finished products slowly cool off. Breslow's creations, one-of-a-kind art marbles, sell for $20 to $150, but he also sells lots of machine-made marbles (a million or more) that cost a whole lot less.

A woodworker since he was a kid, Breslow started making marbles after he had trouble finding them for the old-fashioned wooden games he was making. Marbles now make up 75 percent of his business.

Most of the marbles for sale are machine-made. A few years ago, Breslow was looking for Bumblebees and Boy Scouts, marbles named for their colors. His search led him to a company in West Virginia, where he ordered 8,500 marbles (or so he thought). When the order arrived, it contained 85,000 marbles, and a new career was born.

If you want to tour the marble-ous factory and buy a glow-in-the-dark Moon Marble T-shirt, stop by the store at 600 East Front Street in Bonner Springs. Call (913) 441-1432 or check out www.moonmarble.com for more information.

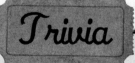

Trivia

Before Prohibition, Kansas had more than 7,000 acres of vineyards, and at one time, Missouri and Kansas produced 86 percent of the country's wine.

Stumps Me: A Retirement Home for Tree Stumps
Council Grove

Council Grove has not one, not two, but three celebrated tree stumps. The town's name, in fact, came from one of the stumps back when it used to be a 70-foot tree. Called Council Oak, the tree with the 16-foot diameter was the official "council site" for the Osage Indians. When government officials decided to seek permission for settlers to pass safely through Osage land, they scheduled a pow-wow under the tree in August 1825. The big cheese of the Osage, in return for $800, signed a treaty agreeing not to disturb stagecoaches, wagon trains, or others heading down the Santa Fe Trail. Unfortunately, the tree was knocked down by wind in 1958, but its stump is still there, still attracting visitors.

Visitors also can see Post Office Oak, which is also nothing but a stump as of 1990, when the 300-year-old bur oak unfortunately bit the dust. In its heyday, it served as the official post office for travelers on the Santa Fe Trail. Between 1825 and 1847, travelers going one way left mail in a hole at the bottom of the tree for travelers going the other way. Letters must have been addressed something like, "George Custer, Council Grove Oak."

Which brings us to the third famous Council Grove stump. It's called Custer Elm, and it too is no longer a "real tree." It's named for General George Custer who, before his ill-fated rendezvous at Little Bighorn, owned the land it sits on.

Although these stumps are nothing but a shadow of their former selves, they are being treated to a fine retirement under fancy canvases in this historic city on the old Santa Fe Trail. You can pick up a map of historic tree stumps at the Council Grove/Morris County Chamber of Commerce and Tourism, (800) 732-9211, www.council-grove.com. Council Oak and Post Office Oak are on Main Street, at the 300 and 100 blocks, respectively. Custer Elm is 4 blocks south on Neosho Street, also known as Highway 177.

★ ★

Trivia

Hermit's Cave is a tiny rock cave built by Italian religious mystic Giovanni Maria Augustini, who lived there in 1863 before walking 500 miles along the Santa Fe Trail to New Mexico.

In-law Problems

Hiawatha

In the middle of Mount Hope Cemetery in Hiawatha, Kansas, is an extravagant quarter-million-dollar memorial to John Milburn Davis and his wife, Sarah. The memorial, with its eleven life-size Italian marble statues of John and Sarah, attracts nearly 30,000 visitors a year.

Commissioned during the Depression by Davis himself, the expensive cemetery plot was meant to honor Sarah. Or that's what Davis claimed if anybody questioned why all these lavish Carrara marble statues were coming to Kansas from Italy. But naysayers insisted Davis built it to spite his wife's family. Let's just say Sarah's dad wasn't overjoyed when his daughter decided to marry the former San Francisco trolley driver.

Before Sarah died in 1930, the Davises lived a frugal lifestyle. They farmed their 260 acres, saved their money, and refused to buy much of anything, even though they had no children to whom they could leave an inheritance.

After Sarah's death, Davis had a change of heart. He moved the simple Davis headstone from his wife's grave to his brother's plot on the other side of the cemetery. Within a year, the handcrafted marble statues began arriving, each depicting Davis and his wife at various stages in their life together. Davis sent waist, height, hip, and shoe measurements to the Italian sculptors so they'd be realistic in every

★ ★

way. The eleven marble and granite statues include a winged angel version of Sarah in prayer, an empty overstuffed chair, and figures of Davis without his left hand, which he lost to infection.

Needless to say, city fathers were dismayed. They begged Davis to reconsider his lavish spending and to invest instead in the town,

Family Feud: John Davis didn't want his money to go to his in-laws when he died, so he "plotted" to spend it on this $250,000 memorial.
HIAWATHA CHAMBER OF COMMERCE

14

which at that time didn't even have a hospital. The eccentric Davis refused, choosing to spend every last penny on the elaborate memorial. He visited the site weekly, and often personally greeted tourists before his death in 1947.

Despite his refusal to listen to city fathers, Davis's extravagant memorial has benefited the community. Articles have appeared in *Newsweek, People,* and *Life* magazines, and people troop to Mt. Hope Cemetery from around the world.

To pay your respects to Davis and his wife, go east on Iowa Street in Hiawatha from US 73.

Trick or Treat

The oldest Halloween parade in the world was started in 1914 in Hiawatha. Mrs. John Krebs, president of the Hiawatha Garden Club, couldn't bear one more year of watching all those costumed trick-or-treaters tramp though the town's flower beds. Rather than fight them, she decided to throw a parade. City fathers pooh-poohed the idea, said it was ridiculous. But it worked, and now, nearly a century later, the parade holds the distinction of being the oldest continuously running Halloween parade in the world. Every year, an effigy of Mrs. John Krebs is pulled through the parade in an antique car with a convertible top.

The parade starts at 7 p.m. every October 31, unless Halloween falls on a Sunday, in which case it's held October 30.

Starting at the Bottom
Kansas City

John Woods's son Timmy had good reason to send his dad nutritional energy drinks. He's eighty, after all, and has undergone five operations in the last few years. But rather than drink the cases of Boost that Tim, one of six kids, shipped from Omaha, Woods turned them into a team of twenty-four oxen, 18 feet long. The red plastic bottles, still full (sorry, Timmy), made a splashy art medium.

Of course to John Woods, a former aerospace engineer, pretty much everything is a potential art medium. His first medium, in fact, was the junk he dug up from the bottom of West Lake in LA's Mac-Arthur Park. He owned an antiques store near the landmark lake, and when city officials drained it in 1973 and 1976 for park remodeling projects, Woods hired local panhandlers to poke through its muddy bed. What they brought back was a century worth of treasure: hundreds of watches, rusty tools, antique toys, corroded trolley tokens, old hotel keys, guns, knives, brass knuckles, and rusty bullets.

"The police confiscated some of the weapons for a while," he says.

Woods patiently cleaned, polished, and cataloged the thousands and thousands of items until one day he started gluing them together, creating whimsical sculptures and three-dimensional maps.

"People call me an artist, but the only thing I know about art is that I'm not interested in it. The only reason I'd ever go to an art opening is if I had a piece in it," he says.

Well, he has been to several art openings with pieces and shows, not only in Los Angeles but also in Kansas City, where he moved in 1996. Art patron Bill Wenzel, recognizing Woods's genius, offered him a house next door to his Wenzel Steel Works.

Although he still has banana boxes filled with refuge from Mac-Arthur Park ("We made at least four trips from Los Angeles," Wenzel says), he has moved on to other projects such as a 6-by-16-foot rendition of John, chapter 17 from the Bible. He carved more than 10,000 letters with metal tabs to mark the verses.

★ ★

King of the hill, bottom of the heap.

Much of Woods's works use visual puns such as his *Name Game* (viewers puzzle out dozens of names from an odd assortment of everyday items) or a large piece in Wenzel's home with dozens of oak letter "E's" in a long pan (Okies from the panhandle) and chairs made of keys (Cherokees).

"His work is magical," said art curator Ginny Brush.

John's *Name Game* and a few other pieces can be viewed at the Grassroots Arts Center, 213 South Main Street (785-525-6118), or Bill Wenzel can arrange a tour. His cell phone is (435) 260-0668.

Swiss Family Schlitterbahn
Kansas City

To this day, Disney's 1960 *Swiss Family Robinson* ranks right up there with *Bambi, Shrek,* and other popular family movies. And ever since it hit the silver screen, kids have pestered their folks to sleep overnight in a tree house. At Schlitterbahn, Kansas City's newest water park, kids can not only catch z's in a tree house, but they can slide from their bunks straight into the adjoining forty-acre water park.

Schlitterbahn's Vacation Village, scheduled to open throughout 2010 and 2011, will not only connect the skyview tree houses via

Captain Jack Sparrow must have lost his pirate map.
TAZ GROUT

slipperslide with the Schlitterbahn Water Park, but kids of all ages
will be able to tube back and forth along canals that connect the tree
houses to Schlitterbahn's riverwalk shopping and entertainment district. There's even indoor skydiving.

Coming to Kansas in several phases, Schlitterbahn also features an
uphill water coaster, a lazy and not-so-lazy river, and the world's largest tidal wave river. Eventually, it will be 360 acres with more than
four miles of man-made rivers.

Schlitterbahn is located at 9400 State Avenue, off I-435 at exit 13,
(913) 334-5200, www.schlitterbahn.com.

Chug-chug Woo-woo—Here Comes Food
Kansas City

There's no mistaking a ready order at Fritz's Union Station in Kansas
City, Kansas. You'll hear the toot-toot, ring-ring, and chug-a-lug of a
miniature railroad car circling the restaurant.

When the train arrives at your table—with burgers, fries, and
cherry malts in tow—your order will be dumped off and lowered to
the table on a miniature elevator.

Fritz Kropf invented the train back in 1970, not because he had a
special affinity for railroads but because he was tired of employees
calling in sick. Using a 12-volt heater motor from an old car, Kropf
designed an engine that would circle his restaurant, deliver food, and
eliminate the need for waitresses.

Although he now has two patents (on the train itself and on the
elevator), it took a while to work the bugs out. The first week, Fritz's
newfangled invention accidentally overturned a bowl of chili on a
customer's favorite dress.

Fritz didn't conceive his time-saver as an actual train until customers started bringing in railroad memorabilia. The casual drive-in now
sports a wide variety of train mementos, from wooden cabooses and
train lanterns to railroad station signs. All employees wear red engineer's scarves, customers get paper engineer hats, and the jukebox

Would you like fries with that?
MARY BETH HOWE-BERNHARDT

plays Glenn Miller's "Chattanooga Choo Choo."

Today, Fritz's is run by his youngest son, Fred, and his wife, Mary. Carrying on a long family tradition (the restaurant opened in 1954), Fritz's still serves the classic burgers with fresh grilled onions and funny names like the Kitchen Sink.

To try the Gen-Dare burger, a popular choice that comes with crunchy hash browns, grilled onion, and melted cheese right on the bun, stop by Fritz's Union Station at 250 North 18th Street. Call (913) 281-2777, www.fritzskc.com.

★ ★

Popeye Would Be Proud

Lenexa

Every year, on the first Saturday after Labor Day, the Lenexa Historical Society makes the world's largest spinach salad. Using pitchforks and 150 pounds of fresh spinach, 600 fresh mushrooms, 100 cloves of garlic, 12 jars of bacon bits, 75 cups of vinegar, and 50 cups of salad oil, this gigantic salad is mixed in a plastic swimming pool.

Plate-size servings are available at Lenexa's annual Spinach Festival. Once known as the Spinach Capital of the World, Lenexa is where Belgian farmers in the 1930s took their spinach to be shipped to New York and Chicago canneries.

Other zany events at the festival have included Spinach Eve polka dancing, green rock skipping, a dog and owner look-alike competition, and a briefcase throw, which was once profiled by John Madden as one of America's craziest sports.

The festival is held on the first Saturday after Labor Day at Sar-Ko-Par Trails Park, 87th Street and Lackman Drive. Phone (913) 541-8592 or visit www.ci.lenexa.ks.us.

The Sunflower Will Come Out, Tomorrow

Lenexa

Tourism in Lenexa suffered a devastating blow in 2008 when Bill Nicks, former director of Lenexa Parks and Recreation, retired and took one of the city's prime tourist attractions along with him. His personal collection of sunflower memorabilia, the world's largest, was proudly displayed in his office at the Lenexa Community Building. Upon his retirement, all 3,556 items—ranging from a seventy-pound manhole cover ("I can't divulge where I acquired this piece, but I will say I wouldn't advise jogging in Topeka at night," says Nicks) to a sunflower-shaped flyswatter—were boxed up and taken home to the family basement, a sobering development that realized his wife's biggest fear.

Of course, she should shoulder part of the blame. She's half the reason he started the collection in 1998.

**Bill Nicks shows off his "onliest" collection
of sunflower memorabilia.**
BILL NICKS, JR.

"We noticed we had lots of items with sunflowers around the house—hats, mugs, napkins. One of us said, 'I wonder how many things have sunflowers on them,'" Nicks explains.

Since then, the collection blossomed and Nicks became a sunflower celebrity.

"My collection has certainly received more notoriety than it deserves," says Nicks, who has appeared on a General Mills billboard, in *Smithsonian* magazine, and on live remotes for the F/X Collectibles channel.

★ ★

Some of his most unique items are the sheet music for the 1949 Billboard chart topper "Sunflower," which was sung by Frank Sinatra; an Oscar Wilde perfume card from the 1880s (Wilde considered the sunflower his signature flower); a sunflower ashtray from Paris; and sunflower seeds from Japan.

The good news about the world's largest collection of sunflower memorabilia ("My wife calls it the onliest collection," Nicks says) is Nicks still gives presentations. To request your own private sunflower presentation, e-mail Nicks at historykc@gmail.com.

Too Bad Lawrence Welk Didn't Know about This
Manhattan

When Earl Slagle was ten, he got a royal tanning for taking the wheel off his Uncle John's new Ford automobile.

It was an innocent mistake. He just wanted to know how the newfangled contraption worked. In sixty-some years, Slagle's curiosity hasn't waned. Only now, instead of taking things apart, he puts them back together. Or creates them from scratch.

For thirty-five years, Slagle worked at Kansas State University, first in the horticulture department, then in forestry. Whenever professors needed something—say a temperature-controlled growth chamber for watermelons, for example—they called on Slagle, who could always figure out a way to build whatever they needed.

After he retired, Slagle turned his attention to his own creative projects. He has made everything from 2-by-3-foot Plexiglas bubble machines to catapults for hedge apples. He has painted dead apricot trees orange and stenciled still-growing apples with K-State's Wildcat logo. After someone gave him 256 CD-ROMS (probably offering 256 hours of AOL or something), he made what he calls "a high-tech tree" with eight arms, 256 hanging CDs, and a glow that would give Francis During's reflector house a run for its money.

"I always have two or three projects going," says Slagle. "I couldn't finish all my projects if I live to be a hundred."

He and his wife, Wanda, have a beautiful home in the hills over-looking Manhattan. Earl designed it so there's no sun heating up the house in the summer, but an abundance streaming in during the winter.

To see Slagle's work, drive by his home at 3221 Stagg Hill (you'll recognize it by all the moving sculptures and Burma-Shave artwork) or visit the Grassroots Art Center in Lucas (213 South Main Street), where one of his four bubble machines is displayed. Phone (785) 525-6118.

A Bug's Life
Manhattan

Ladies and gentleman, the thoroughbreds are coming 'round the bend. It looks like . . . oh, my stars . . . it looks like they're neck and neck. Will it be Lane Number One's German Cockroach (*Blattella germanica*) with the two dark stripes, or will it be Lane Number Two's Oriental Cockroach (*Blatta orientalis*) that almost looks black as it streaks by the stands?

At the K-State Insect Zoo in Manhattan, entomologists stage what can only be called the Triple Crown of Cockroach Racing. These derbies, designed to educate and, well, inspire, are held throughout the year at the Old Dairy Barn turned Insect Zoo. The K-State Insect Zoo, one of only a few in the world, contains more than 1,000 wriggling, squirming insects, all cared for by a full-time zookeeper.

No need to bring the Raid! Most of the zoo's six-legged denizens are caged in Plexiglas or in cabinet drawers in the demonstration kitchen, where insect cooking demonstrations take place. The Insect Zoo, which consolidates a succession of live insect exhibits scattered around the campus since the school opened in 1863, also has a walk-through tropical rain forest. No word on whether or not the derbies serve mint juleps.

To bug out, stop by 1500 Dennison Avenue, (785) 532-2847, www.ksu.edu/butterfly.

★ ★

Rest in Pieces
Maple Hill

When Sarah Ann Oliver died on January 2, 1923, her relatives figured they'd save money on the gravestone by pouring it themselves. Unfortunately, they overlooked one small thing. When they took the stone out of the mold, the letters that looked so perfect in the casting were reversed. So dear old Sarah Ann had to go to the grave with her stone printed backward.

You can find her modest, budget-conscious stone just west of the church that sits in the middle of the Maple Hill Cemetery. Take a mirror to read it. Take exit 341 off I-70, and go left at the intersection. The cemetery is at 2301 South 34th Street.

**The last time the Oliver family insisted
they could "do it themselves."**
PAM GROUT

★ ★

Can I Have Your Autograph before You Starve and Get Eaten by Your Fellow Pioneers?

In May 1846, a west-ward-bound wagon train got delayed for five days while waiting for the swirling floods of the Big Blue River to calm down. This late-May reprieve gave the Donner-Reed party just enough time to carve their names into the sandstone rocks near Alcove Springs. Today, Alcove Springs, as the ill-fated pioneers named this scenic river valley, is not only on the Historic Register but also has 5 miles of trails through native grasses and wildflowers.

Squirrels in Black
Marysville

Drive in any entrance to this prosperous river town and you'll see big signs proclaiming it "The Black Squirrel City." Indeed, coal black squirrels have the run of the town, with a city-proclaimed right-of-way on any street, alley, or railroad track. In 1972, city commissioners made black squirrels the official town mascot, granting them immu-nity from all traffic regulations, freedom to trespass on all county property, and the first pickings of the town's black walnuts.

★ ★

No one knows for sure where the huge population of black squirrels came from, but the most persistent legend claims a local hooligan unlocked a cage of the dark rodents from a carnival of Gypsies who camped in City Park for three nights in the 1920s. Evidently, they breed like rabbits, because today most of the town's squirrel population is jet black.

However they got there, there's no question the squirrels are here to stay. Needless to say, the "Black Squirrel Song" is the official town anthem. It goes like this:

Lives in the City Park

Runs all over town

The coal black squirrel will be our pride and joy

Many more years to come.

Marysville is located at the intersection of US 36 and US 77.

That Was a Sorry Sermon

In 1915, George Morton Field, pastor of the church in Muscotah, agreed to pay his mistress, Gertie Day, $2,000 if she'd leave town without breathing a word of her pregnancy. Panicky that she might try to blackmail him anyway, he wired dynamite to go off when she came to the church to pick up her bribe. The plan worked. It killed Gertie, leveled the church, and left but one shred of evidence: Field's sermon from the week before that he'd used to wrap around the dynamite. He was convicted and sent to prison.

★ ★

That's One Heck of a Piece of Corn

Ottawa

From Paul Bunyan to King Kong to "the one that got away," tall tales have always been popular in America. One photographer from Ottawa was particularly good not only at telling tall tales, but at

Who says everything's bigger in Texas?
FRANKLIN COUNTY HISTORICAL SOCIETY, INC.

"proving them" with his photographic postcards. William H. "Dad" Martin made his fortune selling what are known today as exaggeration postcards.

After stumbling across some new photography tricks in 1908, Dad started the Martin Postcard Company, which sold more than seven million postcards with such photos as men riding saddled roosters, pumpkins uprooting farmsteads, and ears of corn that required flatbed trucks for transportation to market.

By superimposing two black-and-white photos and coming up with funny captions such as "Shipping a few of our peaches" or "Harvesting a profitable crop of onions in Kansas," he captured the attention of state Secretary of Agriculture Foster Dwight Coburn, among others. Coburn, who was already bragging about Kansas's prowess in the fields, sent out hundreds of thousands of news releases claiming such facts as "Kansas sheep have the heaviest fleece" and "Kansas farmers grow more wheat than Belgium and Holland combined."

Soon a rivalry was started with Texas, and tales went something like this: Yeah, Texas grows some big sunflowers, but the sunflowers in Kansas are so big that one night a farmer tied his cow to a sunflower, came out the next day, and thought he'd lost her . . . until he looked up and saw the cow dangling 40 feet up in the air, the distance the sunflower had grown that night.

Martin's whimsical postcards were sent as proof to disbelievers everywhere.

To see some of Dad's giant peaches, stop by the Old Depot Museum at 135 West Tecumseh Street in Ottawa (785-242-1250) or send electronic versions of the postcards at www.old.depot.museum. The Kansas State Historical Society's Center for Historical Research at 6425 Southwest Sixth Avenue in Topeka (www.kshs.org) also curates an impressive collection.

★ ★

Paris, Kansas?

Rosedale

My friend Ron spent several thousand dollars flying to Paris to see the
Arc de Triomphe. He could have saved himself the trip, the money,
and the jet lag if he'd only gone to Rosedale, Kansas, instead. Over-
looking Turkey Creek, only a short hop, skip, and a jump from the
home he shares with his wife, Jana, is a scaled-down but just as
pretty version of the famous Paris landmark.

Not that locals pay much attention. Soon after it was built in 1924
to honor World War I soldiers, the WPA came up with a project that
required building a 22-foot wall only 82 feet away. Unfortunately,
the wall had no stairs, making it next to impossible to get to the
Rosedale Monument. In fact, the groundbreaking drew more people
and attention than the monument's dedication twelve months later.
Weeds and trees soon overtook the 34-foot arc, which was designed
by J. Leroy Marshall, a Rosedale architect. Marshall had made
sketches of the "real thing" while serving in the American Foreign
Legion.

Lucky for you, the Rosedale Monument has now been restored
to its former glory. You can see it at 35th Street and Booth in the
Rosedale section of Kansas City.

They'll Leave ALL the Lights on for You

Shawnee

Put on your saddle shoes, slick back your hair, and get ready for an
all-electric blast from the past. The Johnson County Museum of History in Shawnee was the first in the country to preserve and interpret a
1950s suburban home. The entire 1,500-square-foot house, complete
with patio and garage, was moved to the museum from its original
site in the Kansas City suburb of Prairie Village. As the centerpiece of
the museum's Seeking the Good Life exhibit, the house portrays the
American dream of owning a home in suburbia. The model home was
originally built in 1954, when Ike was president and every kid owned

"Modern electric living" circa 1954.
JOHNSON COUNTY MUSEUMS

★ ★

That dress! Those glasses!
JOHNSON COUNTY MUSEUMS

a coonskin cap. Kansas City Power and Light built it to showcase the latest innovations in modern electric living, such as electric curtain openers, waist-high electrical outlets, bedside remote controls for the coffeemaker, and televisions hidden behind slide-away pictures.

To experience the good life, visit the home at the Johnson County Museum of History, 6305 Lackman Road. If you call ahead, docents dressed in hats and gloves will give your group a tour. Otherwise you'll have to settle for an ungloved, unchapeaued tour guide. Phone (913) 631-6709 or visit www.jocomuseum.org.

Truckin' A
Topeka

When Topeka health and zoning officials instructed Ron Lessman to pick up the junk on his family's five-generation farm, he took them at their word. He picked up the front ends of six 1940s and 1950s pickups, stuck their rear axles in the ground with 4,200 pounds of concrete, and turned them into megalith billboards, spray painting his libertarian political philosophy across the doors: RISE UP, FREEDOM (sic) ISN'T LOST.

Built Ford tough.
TAZ GROUT

★ ★

Truckhenge, as his folk art installation is known, has become a cult tourist attraction, with Lessman giddily leading rambling tours of the trucks, his beer-bottle city (made from thousands of old beer bottles, it whistles and hums on a windy day), his 96,000-square-foot Quonset House, and his newest "henge"—boathenge—that he erected from old boat hulls.

"It is a way of saying 'TRUCK YOU' to the local powers that be," says Bob Cutler, a friend and one of the organizers of Truckhenge's annual free music festival, where bands play in a natural amphitheater on the fifty-six-acre farm. "Truckhenge is Topeka's counter-balance to Fred Phelps and his pickets."

As for Lessman, he's just doing his art.

"I believe in recycling," Lessman says of his penchant for collecting license plates, fossils, rocks, beer bottles, bumpers, and hubcaps and turning them into comical artwork.

Or more useful applications. When the field reviewers from Roadside Attractions asked him if the trucks could be used as a solar calendar, he thought for a moment and said, "Well, the sun does come up here."

If you want to join Lessman and his nose-thumbing, he's at 4124 Northeast Brier Road, Topeka, right inside the gate of Victory Sand and Gravel, (785) 234-3486.

Bone To Be Wild
Topeka

Paleontologists piece together bones to create skeletons. Steve Gray, owner of Kickstart Saloon, a Topeka biker bar, pieced together bones he picked up on his motorcycle jaunts around Kansas to make a full-size Harley-Davidson.

The Palencyclist is in a glass-enclosed display at Kickstart. According to the museum-like exhibit, it was made from 10,000 cow and other animal bones and determined, in a meticulous analysis of beer

★ ★

and alcohol spillage, to be the world's oldest motorcycle. Gray claims it was found in 3025 b.hd. (Before Harley-Davidson).

When asked what compelled him to make the unique motorcycle, Gray answers honestly, "Too much beer."

Kickstart, which also has 150 bras and memorabilia from various motorcycle wrecks on display, is open noon to 2 a.m. seven days a week at 2521 North Kansas Avenue, 1 block north of US 24. Phone (785) 296-9295, www.kickstartsaloon.com.

Nothing quite like the feel of wind through your hair, bugs in your clavicle . . .

Only You Can Prevent Forest Fires

Let's hope the Feds don't catch wind of Blind Tiger Brewery's award-winning Smoky the Beer. While we're not sure if it violates the Smokey Bear Act of 1952 that takes Smokey out of the public domain and mandates all royalties go for education on forest fire prevention, we do know this amber-colored, smoke-flavored beer deserves all the medals it has pulled down since John Dean invented it in Blind Tiger's on-site brew kettle and fermentation tanks. Blind Tiger, named for the Prohibition tradition of hanging stuffed tigers to alert customers to the availability of illegal hooch, brews six hand-crafted, cleverly named ales. Check them out at 417 Southwest 37th Street, Topeka, (785) 267-BREW, www.blindtiger.com.

No Shirt, No Pants, No Problem
Topeka

At Lake Edun, a ten-acre lake southwest of Topeka, guests canoe, hike, swim, and play volleyball in nothing but their birthday suits. There's great freedom, members of the private club claim, in not being judged or valued for your designer duds. And besides, there's a lot less to pack for a weekend trip.

Every few years, this Kansas branch of the AANR (American Association for Nude Recreation) sponsors a one-act play competition. And, yes, many of the plays are performed in the nude, although the theme for the rousing play festival (entries come in from playwrights all over the country) is "body acceptance." Prize for the top play (2009's winner was *Alarmed* about a fire alarm and a girl in a shower) is $500.

The revealing plays are staged at the Hussey Playhouse at the Topeka Performing Arts Center.

For more information about Lake Edun (*nude* spelled backward), contact Webb and Julie Garlinghouse at Box 1982, Topeka 66601, www.lakeedun.com.

They Had To Be Good for Something
Topeka

Environmentalists tell us pull tabs from aluminum cans are dangerous to squirrels, chipmunks, and other curious animals. Herman Divers came up with the perfect solution: He saved the metal rings from beer and pop cans, connected them, and turned them into art.

The retired hospital handyman made everything from a full-size VW bug to a full-size suit of clothes, complete with shoes and umbrella, for both himself and his wife. And maybe there's something about living in the state's capital, because, like Steve Gray, he also made a full-size Harley-Davidson. But instead of bones, Divers's is made out of 179,200 pull tabs.

Divers's unique affinity for pull tabs began in the early 1980s, when he asked the hospital's snack bar attendant if she'd start saving them.

"I told her I was going to make a bedspread. She thought I was crazy," Divers says. "I just figure you can't get into too much trouble when you're working."

Now that it's getting harder to find enough pull tabs, Divers has branched out into buttons. He has made a lamp, a full-size horse, a chair, a button bassinet for his granddaughter, and the cane he uses to walk with.

To view the amazing pull-tab motorcycle and car (he and his grandson can sit in it), head to the Grassroots Art Center in Lucas, 213 South Main Street, (785) 525-6118, wwwgrassrootsarts.net.

(See photo on next page.)

Does this constitute drinking and driving?
JON BLUMB.COM

★ ★

Four Square and More than Seven Years Ago . . .

Troy

On September 21, 1959, *Life* magazine had the audacity to nickname Kansas "Squaresville, USA." The iconic magazine, in a piece contrasting middle-class Americans to the "beatniks" of Venice, California, showed clean-cut Kansans gazing at family photo albums, visiting grain elevators, and swimming in the local pool. Sure, we do all those things in Kansas, but so do people in California, Florida, and New York.

In the end, the *Life* article proved two things. One, the media is extremely powerful. And two, it doesn't always get things right. In fact, about the only square thing in Kansas is the pie that Eugenie Ricklefs serves at her Home Place Restaurant in Troy. A former school

Pi(e) squared.
JAMES S. DICK

★ ★

cook, Ricklefs makes more than twenty-five types of square pie (rhu-berry, apricot, and peanut butter meringue, to name a small sampling) in 12-inch by 20-inch pans, a tradition she originally dreamed up for school kids who she felt deserved better than frozen pies, lunchroom policy until she came along. Open for lunch only (11 a.m. to 2 p.m, every day except Saturday), the former funeral home also dishes up daily specials and homemade soups. Be sure to add your autograph and story to the cozy restaurant's roll-out signboard mounted on a rolling pin at 102 South Liberty Street, (785) 985-3800.

Indian Giver
Troy

What used to be a ten-story bur oak has morphed into an Indian. Thanks, of course, to a chainsaw and a Hungarian-born sculptor who made it his life mission to carve statues of Native Americans in all fifty United States. Peter Wolf Toth calls the monuments he carves out of native trees and stones "The Trail of the Whispering Giants." Toth, who grew up in a family of eleven children, fled Hungary in 1956. He says he has always felt a kinship with the Native Americans who, like his countrymen, were tortured and abused. The statue in Troy, which he started May 1, 1978, took seven months to carve. The statue's feathers, neck brooch, and headband are composites of those worn by Native Americans from the Kickapoo, Pottawatomie, Iowa, and Sac and Fox tribes that inhabited the area before the White Man.

Toth's statue can be seen on the south lawn of Courthouse Square at Main and Walnut.

Happy Birthday(s) to You
Valley Falls

Joan Rivers should be grateful she doesn't live in Valley Falls. Thanks to the "birthday lady," it's pretty much impossible to lie about your age. If you're one of the 1,200 residents of this tiny town, Diane

Smoke signals.
JAMES S. DICK

★ ★

Heinen, aka the birthday lady, knows when your birthday is. She keeps it in her special "little black book," and when that fateful day arrives, Heinen not only knows it, she announces it in giant block letters for all the world to see.

Heinen gets up 365 days a year—rain, sleet, or snow—to drive her white Cadillac to Valley Ag on the main drag of Valley Falls. Using white shoe polish that she special orders from Texas (the regular kind doesn't last), she writes HAPPY BIRTHDAY and lists the name of every single person having a birthday that day. Her list also includes former Valley Falls residents, even if they now live in Timbuktu.

The time-honored tradition started more than twenty years ago when Dorothy Billings wrote HAPPY BIRTHDAY to a friend of hers on the plate-glass window of her family's business. Although it started as a joke, it's grown into a community tradition. When Billings retired, Heinen asked if she could take over. Not only does it build community spirit, "It's a great way to get free beer on your birthday," agree residents.

To find out whose birthday it is today, drive by Valley Ag at 301 Broadway.

Setting the Record Straight
Wamego

If you want the straight scoop on Dorothy, Toto, and the Tin Man (as opposed to the Hollywood version that MGM cemented into our consciousness in 1939), it's high time for a skip through Wamego's Oz Museum.

Oh sure, the museum has the classic movie playing in one of the exhibit areas and displays one of only three remaining flying monkey props (it's made from rubber and has a pipe cleaner tail), but it also has galleries honoring the thirteen other Oz books L. Frank Baum wrote, the earlier silent films (one even starred Oliver Hardy of Laurel and Hardy fame as the Tin Man), and board games, toys, and other

We're off to See the Wizard

Most towns the size of Wamego have let big-box stores bully their way in and steal the show. But thanks to some enterprising business minds, Wamego has managed to keep Lincoln Avenue, its main drag, bustling with locally owned, Kansas-themed businesses. Here's the short list of locally owned products:

Toto's Tacoz serves yellow bricks (burritos smothered in cheese) and courage hot sauce for those with the galls of the Cowardly Lion.

Oz Winery blends such award-winning wines as Run Toto Run, Professor Marvel's Ruby Red, and Witch in a Ditch.

And as for that 9-mile haul from I-70, Wamego simply renamed it "The Road to Oz" in honor of its Oz Museum.

"Most people rely on life's default setting," says Clark Balderson, a longtime Wamego entrepreneur who has built several companies from scratch. "We don't do that in Wamego. We do things our way. We work hard, we think outside the box, and we know that we can make about anything happen."

memorabilia that came out long before MGM got a hold of the Oscar-winning script.

The unique Oz collection, loaned to the museum by Friar Johnpaul Cafiero, a Franciscan priest, has more than 25,000 pieces and is considered one of the world's largest.

To find out the answers to such questions as why the color of Dorothy's slippers was changed from silver (in the book) to red (in the movie), visit the museum at 511 Lincoln, call (866) 458-TOTO, or visit www.ozmuseum.com.

★ ★

Pome on the Range

I don't know how New York got the nickname "The Big Apple," but whoever coined the term had obviously never been to Wathena, Kansas.

Back in the 1920s, a couple of brothers named Hunt built a two-story wooden apple 3 miles west of Wathena on US 36. This architectural wonder had a ballroom in back, a gas station out front, and groceries and other sundries in between.

When the popular landmark burned down during the Depression, the people of northeastern Kansas were devastated. The Hunt brothers felt obligated to rebuild it, this time a bit larger. When it burned down for the second time on July 12, 1940, the brothers took it as a sign and let "The Big Apple's" memory ease into history's annals.

Shoe-be-doo-be-doo
Wetmore

A cottonwood tree on John Kissel's Wetmore farm has sole—er, rather hundreds of soles from the sneakers, pumps, clogs, boots, flip-flops, and heels that people have nailed to the old tree. Kissel, who started the "Shoe Tree" in the mid-1980s, leaves a hammer, a can of nails, and a guest book at the base of the tree that has grown adjacent to his family's farm since he was a kid waiting for the mailman under its branches. The tree has even inspired a song and an ode to its many glories.

"We get people from all over. They come in limos, buses, and even on horseback," says Kissel, who at eighty-four can still climb 20 feet into the tree's branches. "We've got a baby shoe, an ice skate, and my old roller skates from 1943."

Shoe Tree Song
Written by Erika Nelson

(Sing along to the tune of "Oh Tannenbaum," aka "Oh Christmas Tree")

> Oh Shoe Tree, Oh Shoe Tree
> John Kissel's own attraction.
> Oh Shoe Tree on 80th and V
> How soleful are your branches.
> With cowboy boot, sandals, pumps, and clogs
> Stiletto heels, and old flip-flops
> We nailed 'em to John Kissel's Tree,
> The only one in Kansas!

To add your two laces worth, take Kansas Highway 9 1 mile west of Wetmore, go north on W for 5 miles to 80th. It's 1 mile west at the junction of 80th and V.

The shoe must go on.
JOHN KISSEL

The "Pig" Chill
White Cloud

The piggy bank was invented in White Cloud, a little town of 300 on the Nebraska–Iowa border. In 1913, ten-year-old Wilbur Chapman was devastated when a missionary on leave from a leper colony came to town spouting chilling stories of leprosy's horrible ravages. The missionary, who happened to be an uncle of Wilbur's, claimed chaulmoogra oil could relieve suffering, and that ten kids could be treated for only $25.

Wilbur took it upon himself to help his uncle's lepers. His scheme, a classic capitalist dictum (buy low, sell high) involved a piglet he named Pete. He bought the small pig for $3, fattened him up on slops, sold him for $25, and donated the entire amount to the American Mission to Lepers.

The news of his selfless act got around, and before you knew it, people around the country began saving their spare coins in pig-shaped containers. Thanks to an article in the *Sunday School Times,* a one-page newsletter distributed to hundreds of thousands of churches, more than a million dollars was raised in "pig containers" to fight leprosy. Many of those first piggy banks were known as Pete 2.

The monument to Wilbur Chapman, an obelisk-shaped memorial made of native rock and concrete that was dedicated in 1938, stands just east of the front door of the Community Christian Church on Main Street.

Barn Again
White Cloud and the rest of Doniphan County

The historic barn tour of Doniphan County doesn't have a tour guide or an air-conditioned bus. For that matter, it doesn't even have a bus without air-conditioning. But it does have a brochure that can be picked up at the local chamber of commerce (it's located in the bank) in Troy.

The List Goes On . . .

Also in Doniphan County:

- Fifty ghost towns.

- A lookout along the Missouri River where you can see the four states of Kansas, Iowa, Nebraska, and Missouri. The four-state lookout is 4 blocks from Highway 7, near White Cloud. Follow the signs.

- Wolf River Bob, an ex-Hollywood stuntman, trick bullwhipper, and mapper of the Lewis and Clark Trail, who knows virtually everything there is to know about White Cloud, which he calls "the Switzerland of Kansas."

- A stone where Lewis and Clark, who camped there in 1804, carved their names.

- An entire downtown listed on the National Register of Historic Places and used for the filming of the 1973 movie *Paper Moon.*

This two-color brochure lists several barns that can be driven by, gawked at, and photographed, including the three-story Godfrey Nuzum barn that is built into a bluff; the Kiehnoff barn that has a unique system of louvers for getting air in yet keeping rain and birds out; and the John Fuhrken barn, an octagonal barn that was touted in the late 1800s by the Department of Agriculture as the "wave of the future."

Indeed, back in the days when the Doniphan barns were built, farmers often put more money into their barns than their homes. But today, barns, though still celebrated as an icon of rural life, are being razed just like family farms (3.8 million farms have bitten the dust in the last century).

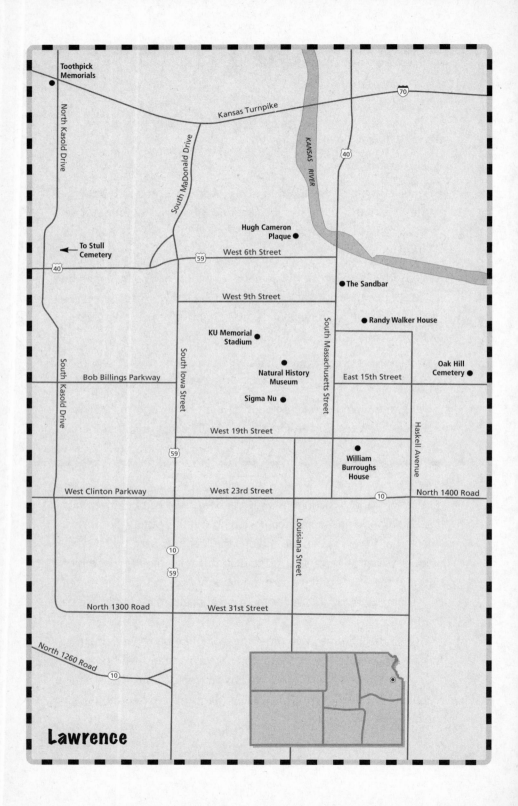

Toothpick
Memorials

North Kasold Drive

Kansas Turnpike

70

KANSAS RIVER

40

South McDonald Drive

Hugh Cameron
Plaque

← To Stull
Cemetery

40   59   West 6th Street

The Sandbar

West 9th Street

South Massachusetts Street

Randy Walker House

KU Memorial
Stadium

Oak Hill
Cemetery

South Iowa Street

Bob Billings Parkway

Natural History
Museum

East 15th Street

South Kasold Drive

Sigma Nu

West 19th Street

Haskell Avenue

59

William
Burroughs
House

West Clinton Parkway   West 23rd Street

10   North 1400 Road

10

59

Louisiana Street

North 1300 Road   West 31st Street

North 1260 Road

10

Lawrence

2

Lawrence

Call it shameless bragging, but my hometown of Lawrence, Kansas, is one cool town. Long a stronghold of individuality, this quirky little burg in the middle of the Bible Belt is the only town in America that was started for no other reason than to spout politics. Folks who didn't think slavery was such a hot idea came here in 1854 to put up their dukes and say, "All people have a right to live as they choose."

Even though Lawrence was burned to the ground by proslavery rabble-rousers who disagreed, that sentiment is the predominant theme to this day. It's why some people think downtown looks like a Halloween party, why you see everything from HONK FOR HEMP signs to Junior League bouffants.

It's why I have the same dentist as William Burroughs, the famous beat poet who chose to live here the last sixteen years of his life. It's why the Lawrence downtown, unlike so many small downtowns, is still vibrant, alive, and attracting such entrepreneurial anomalies as the Waxman candle factory, which has a swing hanging from its rafters, and Local Burger, a hamburger joint that sells burgers made from buffalo, elk, tofu, and, of course, beef—but only beef that's organic and locally grown.

How many towns of fewer than 100,000 can you name that have their own coloring book? Or that put on a community-wide talent show twice a year? Or that host a home tour of the town's old and ugly houses?

★ ★

There's a different parade practically every month. At Christmas, there's a horse parade. Art cars come out in May. April brings an Earth Day parade. March means an all-green St. Patty's parade. Bike parades happen about any month the local "Take Back the Streets" contingent decides to set up couches on Massachusetts Street, the main thoroughfare.

If it sounds like summer camp, that's a pretty fair description. Lawrence is one big summer camp attracting odd characters from all over the world. Practically any one of its 80,000 inhabitants could qualify for a listing in this book. Maybe that's why Hugh Beaumont, the actor who played Leave It to Beaver's straitlaced Ward Cleaver, left town when he was still in high school.

Of course, the Convention and Visitors Bureau, which loves to roll out the town's honors, tends to bring up the fact that the National Trust for Historic Preservation includes Lawrence in its dozen distinctive destinations. And when the National Endowment for the Arts ranked cities according to number of artists per capita, Lawrence landed in that list's top twelve.

But for those of us who live here, we like it for all its character and its characters, for the fact that filmmakers like Alyssa Buecker can land HBO contracts for films starring guinea pigs, for the joie de vivre that prompted all of K. T. Walsh's neighbors to add umbrellas to their own yards when the city tried to put a halt to her outdoor art display of umbrellas and bowling ball sculptures, for the statistic that ranks our county third in the country for percentage of Ralph Nader voters.

Sure, we're proud of the University of Kansas and all it has to offer, but we like the fact that in Kansas, we're known as LaLa Land. And we wouldn't have it any other way.

* *

They Shoot Mermaids, Don't They?

As Willie Shakespeare liked to say, "Beauty is in the eye of the beholder." That's certainly the case in Lawrence, where people actually look forward to hurricanes. Of course the hurricanes in Lawrence only last fifteen minutes, involve rum-laced fruit drinks, and abate after drunks dressed in mermaid costumes jump up on the bar and perform the Macarena.

The Sandbar, a cozy cabana just off the main drag in downtown Lawrence, began offering the fake, but ferocious, indoor storms in 2002. Five minutes before the Katrina-clone hits, the local hangout slowly fills with fog and the TV screens flicker to a phony "Channel 69" newscast warning guests of the impending doom. Wind machines and torrential rainstorms complete with lightning, thunder, and driving rain continue until a couple brave volunteers (believe it or not, customers have been known to come to blows over who gets to play the Little, or sometimes not so little, Mermaid) agree to save the day by donning mermaid costumes and dancing on the long wooden bar.

As far as I know, it's the only indoor hurricane in the world. The Sandbar also has huge tanks of exotic fish, tropical decor, a jukebox with lots of songs you know by heart, and a gift shop with clever T-shirts and the funky place's signature costume: bras made from coconuts, what else? In fact, if you can come up with a unique logo to be painted on the coconuts, you win your own bra free of charge.

To experience one of the Sandbar's nightly hurricanes (two on Friday and two on Saturday), show up at their intimate, hurricane-swept bar at 117 East Eighth Street (785-842-0111), or check out their Web cam at www.thesandbar.com.

★ ★

This Spud's for You

Let the sky rain potatoes.

—William Shakespeare, *Merry Wives of Windsor*

John Bowden claims it was Jackie Kennedy who gave him the idea for his annual potato party. This Lawrence New Year's tradition began in 1977 after Bowden heard the former first lady say that the only things she liked to eat were "baked potatoes, caviar, and champagne."

That sounded like a good diet to Bowden, so he told all his friends that he'd provide the baked potatoes if they supplied the caviar and champagne. Now as many as 300 folks show up for the big John Trip Potato Party that starts New Year's Eve day around noon.

"When people ask what time they should come, I always ask, 'Well, how good is your champagne?'" Bowden says.

One year, the potato party revelers downed 131 bottles of the bubbly stuff. For a while, Bowden tied the leftover bottles to a tree outside his door, but then he jumped over a bench, knocked himself out on one of the bottles (it broke, luckily his head didn't), and woke up fifteen minutes later.

"I figured at that point, I should probably quit tying bottles to my tree," he says.

Depending on the weather, the John Trip Potato Party features volleyball, potatoes being launched out of a potato cannon, or cork-popping competitions.

"But the fiercest rivalry has turned into who can bring the best bottle of champagne," Bowden says.

One year, a guest brought a bottle that wholesales for $600. The bottle alone—without the champagne—was worth $300. Luckily, that wasn't the bottle that shattered when Bowden jumped over the bench.

But who, you're probably wondering, is John Trip? "Oh, I just made up that name," Bowden says. But if you look in the Lawrence phone book, there's a listing for Bowden's alter ego. There's even a phone number for John Trip's kids.

If you want to an invitation to the potato party, call (785) 843-7729 and provide the credentials for your champagne.

Is That a Piece of Lettuce Stuck in Your Teeth?

Wait until the Toothpick Holders Collector Society hears about this. Believe it or not, there is an international organization for people who collect toothpick holders. Members (there were 700, at last count) get a newsletter ten times a year and attend a riveting convention each and every August. For their thirtieth anniversary in 2005, they convened in Kansas City to enjoy educational seminars, all-toothpick auctions, and competitive displays.

But what the stellar group didn't know is that in Lawrence, Kansas, not 30 miles from the site of their third-decade gathering, is a woman who "holds" her toothpicks in giant memorials to disaster victims.

Let's take September 11, for example. Like everyone else, Nancy Lawson, the Lawrence grandma with a thing for toothpicks, was devastated by the terrorist attacks. To cope, she came up with the idea of building a memorial using a toothpick to represent each victim. The resulting sculpture, which she calls *Ascension,* was made from 6,000 toothpicks (because 6,000 was an early death toll estimate).

"It's hard to get your mind around that many deaths, around how many people that really is," she says. "I didn't want them to become just another statistic, so this is what I did to honor them, to give it meaning for me. Toothpicks just happened to be the most economical and sensible item I could think of. I said a prayer every time I put a toothpick in place."

Her next memorial, one that took 300,000 toothpicks, was for the victims of the 2004 tsunami. That memorial, a 5-by-2-foot sculpture called *Resurrection,* not only includes toothpicks but tree bark, shells, and strands of wild weeds. It took her an entire year to complete.

"My husband bought so many toothpicks I think the store employees thought we owned a restaurant," she says.

★ ★

"It's my therapy," she says. "It represents something lost, but something that can still be thought of as beautiful."

Nancy's toothpick memorials are in her home at 524 Hurricane Circle. Call (785) 843-5193 if you're interested in paying your respects.

Tooth picky, picky.

★ ★

As You Bike It

Deep in the bowels of East Lawrence lies the Farnsworth Bicycle Laboratory, where bicycle artist Eric Farnsworth turns normal, everyday bicycles into three-wheeled tandems, pedal-propelled wheat grinders, four-tiered Princess bicycles, and couch bikes. Yes, four people can sit on the couch while one unlucky devil does the work.

It's a hobby, but Farnsworth has accepted a few commissions, such as a bike-powered trailer that transports a mower and carries a state commissioner during parades. It was also used once in a wedding.

"Lawrence is knee-deep in bike parts," Farnsworth explains his unique hobby.

He concocted his first bike when he was eight. His father wouldn't buy him one, so he found an out-of-commission three-speed and fixed it on his own. Among his most memorable creations are a bike with a surfboard on top, a bike attached to a shopping cart (it has transported garden tools, groceries, and bed frames), and an exercise bike that actually moves.

Grave Consequences

No matter where you go to law school (UCLA, Harvard, or anywhere in between), you know about John Wesley Hillmon, a Kansas cattle dealer whose body supposedly lies in a wooden coffin in an unmarked grave in Lawrence.

His body, which was dug up several times and photographed in various stages of disintegration, was the subject of six long, drawn-out court battles, two of which ended up in the U.S. Supreme Court. In fact one of our legal system's few exceptions to hearsay evidence—an out-of-court statement that's usually not admissible—owes its very existence to rules put in place after the 1892 U.S. Supreme Court decision in Mutual Life Insurance Co. v. Hillmon.

But maybe I should start at the beginning. John Wesley Hillmon, born in 1848, married a Lawrence girl named Sallie E. Quinn. Soon after their 1878 wedding, they set out in a wagon with a compadre named John H. Brown to claim some cattle ranching land in the southwest United States. They didn't get any farther than Medicine Lodge when Brown accidentally shot his friend in the head with a rifle he was trying to unload from the wagon. Or so he claimed.

Not more than ten days after he was buried, Hillmon's body was dug up at the bequest of the insurance company that held three life

Here lies John . . . or is it Frederick?

★ ★

insurance policies in his name. His body was sent to Lawrence, a 290-mile journey by stage and rail, where a coroner, paid by the insurance company, declared that the body, indeed dressed in Hillmon's clothes, was not Hillmon after all.

Insurance fraud at the time was rampant, and the insurance company, in an effort to nip what they claimed was fraudulence in the bud, decided to fight the claims by Hillmon's widow. Only problem? The company conducted its own fraud in trying to prove that the body was one Frederick Adolph Waters. That's where the exception to hearsay evidence came in. The Supreme Court decided to allow a letter that Waters's "girlfriend" produced, claiming that her twenty-four-year-old beau had joined up with Brown and the two Hillmons shortly past Wichita.

To make a long story short, Sallie Hillmon, after twenty years and six trials, finally got the $25,000, a princely sum in those days, the Federal Rules got Rule 803 (1)(b) with the oft-studied exception to hearsay evidence, and Lawrence got a veritable legal celebrity right in its own Oak Hill Cemetery.

Oak Hill Cemetery is located 1605 Oak Hill Avenue, about 7 blocks east of Haskell on Fifteenth Street.

The Gum Hither Look

In 2003, on the one-hundredth anniversary of the Wright brothers' infamous first flight, the Grassroots Art Center in Lucas staged a "Flights of Fancy" exhibit featuring flying machines made from recycled art. One of the featured attractions was a long-necked bird made from dried grapefruit peels.

The artist who concocted the bird was none other than Lawrence's own Betty Milliken, a yodeling ninety-something self-taught artist who, during her lifetime, made hundreds of pieces of art from grapefruit and orange rinds. Her specialty was portraits—cameos that she fashioned out of not only fruit rinds, but out of caulking compound, bread dough, Styrofoam meat trays, and chewing gum. Yes, chewing

All my children.
NANCY HUBBLE

gum. Her cameos, not more than an inch tall, sometimes sported hats that Milliken knitted, or locks of her own hair. Sometimes she dressed them in photos from magazines. Sometimes she gave them the faces of celebrities—like Joe Namath or Martha Washington. Collectively, her cameos of bubble gum mixed with foot powder and tub caulking were known as "Betty's Children."

How do you make a portrait out of chewing gum?

"Well, first you have to chew the gum," said the colorful Milliken, who passed away August 2005 at the ripe old age of ninety-four. "You gotta get all the sugar out of it. Big Red isn't bad, but Cinnaburst works best."

Born in Detroit, Michigan, to a family of Hungarian immigrants, Milliken grew up really poor (she remembered wearing her dad's barnyard boots that smelled of manure to school) and was a bit of a social outcast. Although she didn't like school, she loved learning. She taught herself art, photography, painting, yodeling, and acupressure, a hobby to which she attributed her longer than usual life. She also played a mean ukulele, banjo, fiddle, guitar, and water xylophone. That's where you set up glasses with varying amounts of water to create different tones.

A sampling of Betty's Children can be viewed at the Grassroots Art Center in Lucas, 213 South Main Street (785-525-6118), www .grassrootsart.net.

The Jane Goodall of Sock Monkeys

Randy Walker charges a buck to get in the door of his house. And that's a bargain. His home on the east side of Lawrence is a veritable museum of American kitsch.

The avid collector, who works as a chef to support his hobby (he also, not surprisingly, runs a booth at the local antiques mall), has collections of bottle cap men, art deco lamps, purses and hats made from bread bags, 3-D religious art, lamps and ashtrays made from deer hooves, postmortem photos, and velvet Elvises. Of course, he

★ ★

also has nonvelvet Elvis memorabilia, including a lock of Elvis's hair, one of his toenails, a fingernail, and pictures of Elvis's underwear that he took last year in Pigeon Forge, Tennessee.

Walker's most recent pursuit is acquiring the world's largest collection of cow hairballs. So far, he has three, the biggest of which is still dwarfed by the Garden City hairball (see chapter 7). But, unlike the Finney County Historical Museum that only gets theirs out when

Say cheese-y! Randy Walker with his collection of sock monkeys (Randy's the one in the middle).

someone asks, Walker's hairballs are all proudly displayed under glass domes.

His most famous collection, however, is his zoo of sock monkeys. He owns more than 350 of the monkeys, which were popular home-made items in the 1950s and '60s. He has monkeys with capes, monkeys with hats, even monkeys with eyes made out of seashells.

"They're like people," Walker says. "Even though they're made from the same basic things, every one is a little bit different. Each one has its own personality."

His favorite Christmas card? What else but a picture of himself surrounded by his monkeys, with the greeting, "From my family to yours."

I'm sorry to report that Walker's cockatiel Raoul, the one who could hum the theme song to *The Andy Griffith Show,* kicked the bucket at the ripe old age of twenty-two (the average cockatiel lives to be fifteen), but Walker still has him in the freezer.

"I'm trying to get somebody to stuff him, but most taxidermists think he's too small," Walker said.

"I collect American junk. If it's in bad taste or ugly, I probably collect it," Walker says of his interesting addiction. "I collect stuff that shows the human spirit. Creativity just bursts out of people. I love it when people are able to make something out of nothing."

If you can spare a buck and want to see a genuinely original home, call Walker at (785) 843-8750. His home is located at 1012 New York Street.

Acres of Socks

Russell Conwell, the founder of Temple University, used to tell a story about a diamond hunter who traveled the world looking for riches. Eventually, he returns home only to discover huge, exquisite diamonds right in his own backyard. A similar story recently unfolded in Lawrence. As you, fine reader of this book, know, Randy Walker's nationwide search for unique sock monkeys has resulted in an

★ ★

Sturgis bound?
PAM GROUT

impressive collection. Entire busloads of tourists have traveled to Lawrence to bask in his sock monkeys' glow.

But lo and behold, during the writing of this third edition, we
discovered a creative genius not a mile from Randy's museum home
that makes not only unique sock monkeys but also sock gorillas,
sock aliens, and sock spiders. Jason Klinknett, the brilliant mind
behind the one-eyed sock aliens, averages a sock creature a week.
And people bring him socks faster than he can thread the needles
he uses to stitch them all by hand. His five-year-old nephew, Enzo,
has a collection that is rapidly gaining on Randy's. And it's not just
kids who enjoy Jason's entourage. His one-of-a-kind sock creatures
reside in homes all over Lawrence. Jason recently branched out into
motorcycles that he builds from chicken bones. Give him a bucket of

✳ ✳

Colonel Sanders and he'll give you a miniature Harley-Davidson. He also makes turtles out of bottles, scorpions and lamps out of bottle caps, and dogs out of bolts.

"He's the master of junk," says Rachael Sheridan, who owns a sock mermaid, a sock octopus, and a sock cat. "He's absolutely brilliant. He inspires creativity in all of us."

Don't Forget to Eat Your Vegetables and Your . . . Art

Most artists use easels and canvas. Stan Herd, an internationally known environmental artist, uses cornfields, tractors, and crops to create his beautiful, albeit large, portraits. He sculpts live, growing crops into designs so huge you can only view them from the air. But

Crop circle conspiracy?
WILL PENDLETON

get high enough and you'll see one-acre Amelia Earharts made from perennial grasses and 160-acre Indian chiefs made from squash, melon, corn, and beans.

Although he calls Lawrence home and has designed many artworks here (Lawrence Riverfront Park sports a giant Stan Herd flowerpot fashioned from rocks), he travels the world creating his one-of-a-kind masterpieces. He once made a giant Absolut vodka bottle the size of sixteen football fields that was featured in magazine ads for the Swedish import.

Herd grew up in tiny Protection, Kansas, and won his first art competition (the grand prize was a whopping $1) when he was in first grade. That award was just the first for the artist, who has been written up by *People, National Geographic,* and *Smithsonian* magazines. After attending art school at Wichita State University, he decided he wanted to think bigger. And bigger indeed he has thought.

His first piece of crop art, created in 1980, was a 160-acre portrait of a peace-loving Kiowa Indian chief named Santana.

Herd's murals can be seen in little towns all over Kansas, including Kingman, Dodge City, Wilmore, Topeka, and Protection. You can call (785) 331-6548, or visit www.stanherdart.com.

Oops . . . Phone Line Stuck in a Tree

Hugh Cameron, known as the Kansas hermit, built a tree house with electricity and a phone. After getting fired from his job in Washington, D.C. (the powers that be didn't approve of his strident abolitionist views), he walked to Lawrence with the first party of twenty-nine hoping to establish Kansas as a free state. That was in 1857. Although he started a newspaper and served in the territorial congress, he eventually foreswore society after a girlfriend jilted him. At fifty-five, he vowed to never cut his hair or beard again.

Cameron lived in a cave for many years, coming out every four years to walk all the way to Washington, D.C., for the presidential inauguration. By 1907, he decided to move closer to town. He built a retirement tree house at what's now Fifth Street and Indiana. The house had a small dining area, a kitchen, electricity, and even a telephone.

While Cameron's tree house was located at what is now Fifth Street and Indiana, there's a plaque honoring this old war fighter and poet's tree house embedded in the sidewalk at Fifth Street and Louisiana (because it was open and available—we're weird here in Lawrence).

Naked Burroughs

He lived in Paris, London, New York, and Tangier. But William Burroughs, the famous poet and artist who is credited with introducing Jack Kerouac and Allen Ginsberg to the beat lifestyle, chose Lawrence as home. Indeed, he lived here longer than he lived anywhere—in a

Burroughs's bungalow.
PAM GROUT

★ ★

modest red frame house where he gardened (one of his typewriters "grew" among the weeds), raised cats, and practiced target shooting. His classic, *Naked Lunch,* published in Paris in 1959 and banned in the United States until 1962, was one of dozens of books he wrote after he accidentally shot his wife in a drunken William Tell accident.

Living in Mexico to escape U.S. drug authorities, Burroughs bragged to his friends he could shoot a wineglass off his wife's head. Unfortunately, he missed, and his wife died almost immediately. If not for that unfortunate accident, he says, he'd have never started writing (he wrote hundreds of books, from *Ticket That Exploded* to *Wild Boys*) and would not have become the much-loved champion of free thinkers everywhere. An admitted homosexual and former heroin addict, Burroughs railed against convention all his life. He still influences the counterculture today. Before his death in 1997, hundreds of "worshippers" came to Lawrence to visit, including Ginsberg, Kurt Cobain, and Deborah Harry.

To see the home Burroughs inhabited from 1981 until a heart attack sent him to Lawrence Memorial Hospital, go by 1927 Learnard Street.

(Red) Dog Day Afternoons

While some people like to exercise with Billy Blanks, Richard Simmons, or Jane Fonda, a huge contingent in Kansas chooses to work out with Don Gardner, a sixty-something ex-Marine with a bullhorn. His nickname is Red Dog, the class is known as Red Dog's Dog Days, and for more than twenty years he has been leading hundreds of believers through laps and push-ups and other strenuous exercises in the sometimes 100-degree Kansas heat.

Gardner and partner Jim O'Connell (his nickname is Punkin—he was born on Halloween) were trainers for the Lawrence High Chesty Lions football team. They grew tired of all the injuries that plagued players at the start of the season, so they launched this hot, brutal workout to get them in shape.

For some unexplained reason it caught on, and now everyone from policemen to waitresses to elementary school kids shows up to be pushed and occasionally sworn at by the infamous Red Dog. In fact, on July 27, 2009, 2,766 people showed up for Red Dog's World's Largest Workout.

The class is free, meets three times a day every summer, and keeps growing every year. To be brutally punished, show up at KU's Memorial Stadium (11th and Maine). But don't say I didn't warn you. www.reddogsdogdays.org

Scary Movie 13?

I live less than 10 miles from one of the Seven Gates to Hell. Or at least that's the rumor. Stull Cemetery, a tiny, run-down graveyard with nothing but a burned-out church, a couple of trees, and headstones with such names as Wulfkuhle and Hildenbrand, sits innocently across from an old bait shop. But on Halloween night, the tiny cemetery opens up a straight path to the red guy himself.

Stull locals—a quiet, peaceful lot—say the rumors are complete gobbledygook. They've erected a fence and given out $100 fines to anybody who tries to prove otherwise. So far, their threats have done nothing to thwart the persistent legends that circulate around the world via the Internet. Some say the devil's child is buried there. Others claim a boy who turns into a werewolf haunts the place. Kurt Cobain of the rock group Nirvana made a pilgrimage to the famous cemetery and tested its most notorious legend: that if you throw a bottle against one of the rock walls, it won't break. Or if it does, says the legend, you're next to join the dead. Well, I can't say I was with Cobain the night he threw his bottle, and I wouldn't know whether or not it broke, but I do know he's not around anymore.

If you dare, Stull Cemetery can be found by taking Sixth Street out to 1600 Street and following it west until you feel chills.

★ ★

Equestrian Elvis Lives On

When the cavalry's burial party arrived two days after General George Custer's ill-fated raid on the Sioux Indians, there was only one living thing left on the Little Bighorn battlefield: none other than a fourteen-year-old steed named Comanche. Even though seven bullet holes pierced his body, Comanche, who got his name when he was struck in the right hind quarter with an arrowhead and supposedly let out a yell just like a Comanche, was still breathing.

The "stuffing" legends are made of.
KU NATURAL HISTORY MUSEUM

He had already survived the Ku Klux Klan, Kentucky moonshiners, and numerous battle injuries. After he was found wounded on the Little Bighorn battlefield, he was taken to Fort Lincoln and nursed back to health. A symbol of American patriotism, for years Comanche made the rounds of parades and festivals all over the country. Like an equestrian Elvis, he was sighted everywhere.

Eventually, Comanche found a permanent home at Fort Riley, Kansas. When he died at the ripe old age of twenty-nine, the Fort Riley cavalry had no idea what to do with the famous steed's carcass. Finally, they contacted the taxidermist at the Natural History Museum, who agreed to stuff him for $400. The cavalry never paid the bill, and the mount, except for a brief exhibit at the Chicago Exposition in 1893, has been in Lawrence ever since.

Even in death, poor Comanche has suffered numerous brushes with danger including an attempt by students to steal him and a near-drowning, which occurred when a goose being thawed in a sink on the floor above plugged the drain, causing water to pour onto the stuffed steed.

Ever since, Comanche has been proudly displayed for all the world to see on the fourth floor of the Natural History Museum at the University of Kansas in a climate-controlled glass case.

The Natural History Museum sits on the university campus just south of the university union, 1345 Jayhawk Boulevard, (785) 864-4450, www.nhm.ku.edu.

Somewhere Over the Bottle

Neither rain nor snow nor sleet can keep Lawrence postman Tom Krause from . . . making and playing musical instruments out of all sorts of odds and ends. He has a bottle flute, for example, that he fashioned out of sixteen different size bottles—from test tubes and vanilla bottles to beer bottles and olive oil containers. He can play everything from "Somewhere Over the Rainbow" to the theme song from *2001: A Space Odyssey* on the bottle flute.

Tom Krause doesn't just separate recyclables—he plays them.
MIKE YODER

* *

He also has instruments made out of salad bowls, trash can lids, and Bundt cake pans. "It has to be the old ones," Krause points out. "The new Bundt cake pans don't have the same resonance."

He plays his odd assortment of instruments in concerts, for school-kids (they love him), and he's even played backup on a CD. Although he has played the guitar since he was in sixth grade, Krause developed an interest in making this unusual music in the early 1990s.

"On second thought, maybe it started back in high school when I played pencils on the dashboard of a '64 Chevy," he says of his unusual hobby.

He once did an installation of pan lids for the University of Kansas.

"I go to the recycling center and instead of putting things in, I take things out," he says.

Krause is quite proud of the fact that he can create four octaves from bottles and two and a half chromatic octaves from mallets that he's made from flatboards and bells.

"If you want the note A, I can tell you just what bottle to look for," he says.

His main message is that "music is for everyone. If we take the mystery out of it, which certainly happens when you're playing 'Amazing Grace' on keyhole saws, everyone will realize they are musical. In an African culture, people don't question whether or not they have musical ability. It's a simple expression of who they are as human beings."

The (Spooky) Sweetheart of Sigma Nu

Even though fraternities are normally "men only," the Sigma Nu fraternity house of the University of Kansas has a frequent female visitor. Her name is Virginia and, well, she's a ghost. When she was living, Virginia was allegedly the mistress of Kansas governor Walter Roscoe Stubbs, who lived in the house when it was the official state mansion.

In 1911, seventeen-year-old Virginia was found hanging from a crystal chandelier on the third floor. This was before Barbara Walters, CNN, and other snoopy reporters, so no one knew for sure whether Virginia, who worked for Stubbs as a servant, killed herself or was murdered by Mrs. Stubbs. All we know is that she was cremated and her ashes were stuffed inside the first floor fireplace. A mysterious plaque in the room that now serves as the fraternity library reads, "The world of strife shut out, the world of love shut in."

Virginia has been getting her vengeance ever since. Members of the fraternity, which took over the house in 1922, report regular disruptions, including rattling doorknobs, heavy footsteps, and flashing lights. In April, the anniversary of her death, she's often seen pacing the floors or sitting on steps.

The frat house is at 1501 Sigma Nu Place, (785) 843-7922.

Bowling with Martha

Columbus discovered the New World. Einstein proposed the theory of relativity. Larry Woydziak, a Lawrence fireman, made it his quest to bowl with Martha in every county in Kansas.

Martha, by the way, is a bag for a mother-of-pearl bowling ball that he bought for $1.95 at a thrift store. It even came with a pair of slightly dirty socks and a 1988 bowling schedule.

As a member of the Kansas Explorers Club, a wild and wacky group that promotes local travel and small-town culture, Woydziak came up with this unusual quest one day at an Explorers conference meeting. He wanted an excuse to see Kansas, so why not do it at the bowling alley?

"Back in the '50s and '60s, the bowling alley was where people in small towns hung out. Thanks to TV and the Internet, many of the small-town bowling alleys are closing up," says Woydziak. "Nowhere are people as friendly as they are in the bowling alley."

Indeed, he did make lots of friends, even became quite a celebrity, drawing huge crowds to his ten-line game in each county. He even created a Web site with a journal called "Larry's Gutter Life."

For a mere $18.61 (the year Kansas became a state), you too can become part of America's most exciting organization. By becoming a Kansas Explorer, you'll receive six newsletters a year that will inform you about such newsworthy events as Larry's last bowl in Sterling (sorry, you missed that one—it was in June 2001), the Kingman farm machinery Christmas parade, and the round hay bale art competition.

You'll learn the top-secret explorer ritual, get a number (I'm Explorer #2098) and a four-color membership card, and have the chance to attend Grand Expeditions, explorer conferences where you might come up with crazy schemes like Larry's. Just don't try to eat biscuits and gravy in every county or jog through every county, because those are already taken. You might even win the LuWonderer Award, a 10-inch limestone fence post (the first one was a Barbie doll) that is passed from member to member.

If you "Dare to Do Dirt," a Kansas Explorers motto, check out the Web site at www.explorekansas.org.

Art Cars Rule

Other than a witty bumper sticker here and there, most of us drive clones, cars that are exact replicas of every other Toyota Camry or Ford Taurus.

Not in Lawrence. This town has a whole fleet of what's known as art cars, cars that express their owners' personalities.

In May, all these one-of-a-kind vehicles come out to strut their stuff in the annual Art Tougeau, a wacky art car parade that celebrates folk art, ingenuity, and community spirit.

If it has wheels and any kind of art facade, it qualifies for entry. Sometimes, that means wheelchairs decorated to look like bananas. Or bikes that look like cows. Once, a grade school rigged up a bunch of wheelbarrows and lawn mowers. Another entry added wheels to a couple of refrigerators. But the art cars usually get the biggest laughs, such as the expensive Jaguar decorated from top to bottom

Instead of mpg (miles per gallon), this
car boasts spg—stares per gallon.

in cookies applied with icing. Or the old Chevy that reflects the sun
with its new coating of thousands of CDs.

Charles Jones, a county commissioner, started the parade back in
1997 after watching a CBS special called *Wild Wheels*. And yes, he's
more than a judge. His art car, although it started as a very normal

★ ★

1983 Ford Escort, now has hundreds and hundreds of trophies glued to its exterior.

Speaking of trophies, students in an art class at the high school rig up wacky trophies (they use twisted wire and old toy parts) to give out at the end of the parade. As one Art Tougeau fanatic said, "It appeals to the exhibitionist in all of us."

To catch the parade, show up on Massachusetts Street the first Saturday in May.

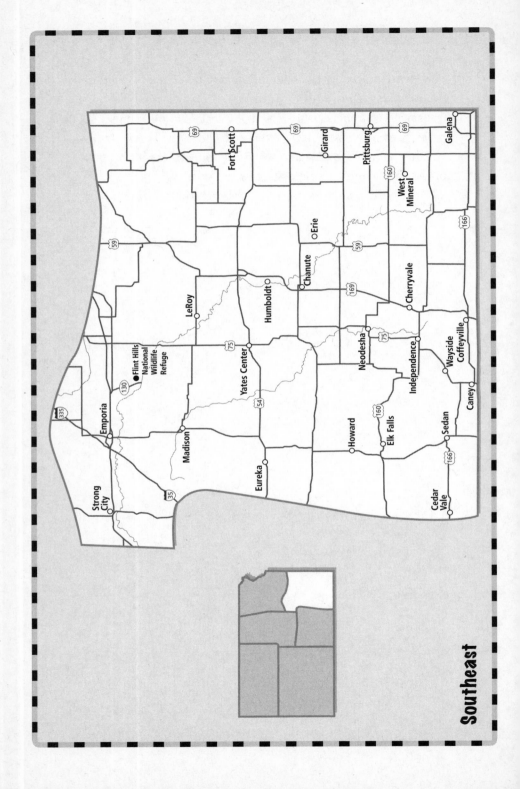

Southeast

3

Southeast

Anybody who thinks *Kansas is backward, conservative, and boring has obviously never opened a history book about southeast Kansas. I dare anybody to malign my state with one of those Archie Bunker–like claims after reading this chapter.*

Not only was there a vegetarian commune near Humboldt in the 1860s, one hundred years before hippies shocked the middle class with such far-out notions, but progressive ideas like eight-hour workdays and the abolition of child labor were hatched in Girard, a small town Jack London once called "a temple of revolution." Not only that, but the world's first protest march was organized in the southeast's Crawford and Cherokee Counties.

The progressive ideas were touted by the Appeal to Reason, *a socialist newspaper that in 1913 had the largest circulation in the country (750,000). The protest march was staged by 6,000 women, wives of coal miners, who took to the streets in 1921 to protest the miserable pay and abominable working conditions their husbands were forced to endure. Girard, by the way, also had an innovative airplane builder who opened one of the country's first airplane factories in an empty lumberyard. Unfortunately, only one of his fourteen designs ever left the ground.*

The southeast also has rare white lions, 13 miles of Route 66, and the world's largest piece of hail. For more fascinating facts about southeast Kansas, read on.

* *

Mom-and-Pop Zoo
Caney

When Tom Harvey was four, he went with his dad, a truck driver, to pick up a load of cattle. They waited and waited until finally the guy who hired them sheepishly sauntered over to the truck to say he was terribly sorry, but his shipment wasn't going to be ready for them after all. He offered to pay him for his time, but Mr. Harvey wouldn't hear of it.

Tame kingdom.
SAFARI ZOOLOGICAL PARK

★ ★

"Well, the least I can do is give your son one of these," he said, walking over to a beat-up El Camino.

He opened the door of the old Chevy and showed them a litter of baby deer that had been born a few weeks earlier in the front seat.

Young Tom giddily picked one out, named him Rudolph (hey, he was four), and took him home, where he made the fawn a bed in his wooden toy box.

"I've had animals ever since," says Tom.

Only now, Tom has exotic animals (seventy some) and his own zoo that he runs with his wife, Allie.

"People think since we're out in Kansas that we probably have a couple chickens, a cow, and maybe some frogs," Tom says. Boy, are they in for a surprise when they pull up to the zoo in tiny Caney. Harvey's ten-acre Safari Zoological Park has black African bear cubs, seven rare white tigers, four black leopards, jaguars, and what could be the only white Barbary lion ever born. People come from China, Australia, and countries most of us have never heard of to see the rare menagerie.

Tom's first exotic, a cougar, was just a pet. But then he got a black African bear cub, a lion, and a mate for the cougar.

People came to visit.

"I was taking so many people out to see them that I couldn't get anything done. I decided that I'd either have to get rid of the people or I'd have to let the people help support the hobby," he said.

Some years, the park that he opened to the public in 1994 does better than others.

In 2008, Sassy, one of the white tigers, rejected her three newborn cubs. She decided she'd had enough of being a mom and refused to let them nurse. Isabella, the Harveys' yellow lab who had just had a litter of pups, adopted them, even took over the nursing details. Before long, Harvey, Allie, and the cubs were on the *Today* show, inking book deals, and fielding calls from all over the world.

"We had just had three tough years. I told my wife, hang on. There's a miracle coming," Tom said.

★ ★

Born free to be nursed by a dog.
TOM HARVEY

The influx of money has allowed him to renovate the park and add a new leopard habitat.

But even with all the improvements, Harvey's zoological park still takes guests on personal guided tours. Anybody who pays the $10 admission is led by Tom, Allie, or one of the volunteers through the park and regaled with funny anecdotes about the animals—when their birthdays are or what they did when they were cubs. Tom has been known to hypnotize the alligators and ride on the backs of lions. If you'd rather feed the animals yourself, you can buy a Ziploc bag of, yes, animal crackers. Up close and personal is the best way to describe it.

To visit the park, take US 75 to old Highway 166 and go east 1½ miles. Phone (620) 879-2885 or log on to www.safaripark.org.

Casting the First (and Second and Third) Stone
Cedar Vale

After Lotus Day suffered a heart attack, he decided to retire from his job as a stonemason. He figured his time was better spent "glorifying God." Some might have thought that sending money to starving kids in Africa would have been enough. But not Lotus Day. He wanted to build a cathedral—a tiny stone cathedral that seats exactly twelve. When he commissioned the oak pews, he told the woodworker, "I want just enough space to seat the twelve disciples."

So far, the disciples haven't shown up. But thousands of other people from every part of the world have. That alone is a miracle, because the church, called Wee Kirk of the Valley, sits in a field off a gravel road that's 6½ miles from the nearest town. You have to climb a barbed wire fence and risk numerous cow patties to get there, but it's worth it. There's a 6-foot marble statue of Christ that was sculpted in Italy, and statues of the Last Supper and Jesus in the Garden of Gethsemane that glow in the morning light. When you close the door to the chapel, recorded hymns begin to play.

Wear your gardening shoes if you plan to visit, because the only way to get there is to follow the gravel road south from Cedar Vale (look for the signs). The good news is that Day made a little wooden step for climbing over the barbed wire fence. Call (620) 758-2867 if you want to schedule a wedding.

★ ★

Lions and Tigers and Scares, Oh My!
Chanute

Chanute's Osa Johnson was the Julia Roberts of the 1920s. When she showed up on the stages of America to sing or talk or show clips from her many safari movies, people came out in droves. Her book, I *Married Adventure,* which was printed on zebra-striped cloth, was a best-seller (*National Geographic* still lists it as one of the best adventure books of all time), and while she was on the vaudeville circuit, she topped fashion magazines' lists of the best dressed.

Of course, no one would have heard of the girl from small-town Kansas if she hadn't married Martin Johnson, a kid from nearby Independence, when she was still sixteen. Martin, who was ten years older, met Osa after returning from a two-year adventure on Jack London's Snark. Martin had responded to London's classified ad for a cook, even though he hadn't the foggiest notion how to cook. He got the job and continued to travel even after the Snark's six-year journey was cut short.

That trip whetted his appetite for exploration and, with new bride Osa by his side, he traveled to the remotest corners of the earth. Not only did the adventurous duo pioneer documentary filmmaking, they also introduced many Americans to new and uncharted worlds. They made nine full-length movies, seventeen short features, and at least a half dozen films for the lecture circuit. Their film *The Cannibal Isles of the South Seas* debuted in 1918 and set box office records across the country.

In 1961, a few years after Osa died of heart failure (Martin had died earlier in a commercial plane crash), Chanute opened a museum in honor of the Johnsons. For a while, donations to the museum were collected in an elephant foot with a board nailed to the top.

The Martin and Osa Johnson Safari Museum contains thousands of artifacts collected by the Johnsons on their five forays into Africa and four journeys to the South Pacific.

Osa's Ark. This zebra-striped Sikorsky S-38 was employed for the Johnson's 1933–1943 "Flying Safari," their fifth and final expedition to Africa.

OSA AND MARTIN JOHNSON SAFARI MUSEUM

Their books and all their full-length safari movies, as well as blow-guns, elephant-foot banks, and 300 pieces of West African tribal art, are on display at the museum, along with handcrafted African jewelry made on-site.

The museum is located at 111 North Lincoln Avenue (Highway 39), 2 miles from US 169. Take Cherry Street to Santa Fe and turn right at the next light. It's open 10 a.m. to 5 p.m., Monday through Saturday and 1 to 5 p.m. on Sunday. Phone (620) 431-2730 or go to www.safarimuseum.com.

Fashionably Kansas

American Eagle Outfitters, the brand preferred by teenagers everywhere, came straight to Kansas when developing a new line for thirty-somethings. Their Martin + Osa brand, launched in 2006 with twenty-eight stores around the country, features clothes inspired by the early Kansas explorers. Although the brand's cashmere sweaters, shorts, and jackets are slightly updated, a Johnson junkie would notice subtle hints throughout the line: belt buckles with 1910, the year the Johnsons married; labels with S-38, the amphibious airplane they used to traverse Africa; or NC-52, their plane's registration number. The Pittsburgh, Pennsylvania, retailer has yet to open a Martin + Osa store in the Sunflower State (although their largest distribution center employs more than 550 in Ottawa), but orders are always available at www .martinandosa.com.

Ax to Grind
Cherryvale

Back in the early 1870s, Kate Bender and her family built a small barn and house near the Osage Mission Trail, a few miles northeast of Cherryvale. A crude sign on the home advertised groceries.

Kate's parents, both in their sixties, kept to themselves, as did their son, John Jr. Kate, however, was just the opposite. She had an outgoing personality and flashing brown eyes, and she was quite popular with local lads. Advertising herself as a "healer," Professor Katie Bender, as she billed herself, passed out flyers claiming she could cure blindness and deafness. The Benders' little home on the trail had a canvas partition. The family bunked on one side; travelers in need of a meal could sit on crude log benches on the other.

There was just one problem with the partition. Behind it, the Benders would wait with axes and sledgehammers and bludgeon their unsuspecting guests to death. There was a trapdoor underneath the bench if for some reason the sledgehammers didn't finish them off. No one missed the first ten travelers who disappeared—or at least they didn't suspect Katie Bender, the great healer, of perpetrating any crime. But when William H. York, a well-known doctor from nearby Independence, disappeared, search parties were sent out. When York's brother and a posse tracked him to Bender's store, Katie admitted that he'd stopped by, but she insisted that he had watered his horse, bought a couple of things, and rode on.

Two weeks later, the Benders' home was deserted. When officials went to investigate, they discovered York's body in a shallow grave in the Benders' orchard. Eventually, they discovered the bodies of ten other victims nearby, including a father and his small daughter, who were all beaten to death with the Benders' tools. The Benders were never seen or heard from again.

To find out more about the murdering family, visit the Cherryvale Museum at 215 East Fourth Street (620-336-3576) or get a copy of Fern Morrow Wood's book, *The Benders: Keepers of the Devil's Inn*.

The book can be ordered by writing to Fern Morrow Wood, Route 2, Box 114, Cherryvale, KS 67335.

Glad They Were Wearing Pads
Coffeyville

Check out the Web site of any weather service and the name of Coffeyville, Kansas, is sure to come up. That's because Coffeyville, a town just a mile from the Oklahoma border, holds the rare distinction of being the very place on the globe where the most gigundus hailstone fell. You've heard hailstones described as golfball-size or pea-size or even softball-size. Well, the hailstone that fell on the west end of Coffeyville on September 3, 1970, was the size of a large rugby ball. It had a 17½-inch circumference and a 7-inch diameter, and it weighed nearly two pounds. And the people of Coffeyville can prove it. Wearing football helmets for protection, they rushed out, snagged the giant hailstone, and stuck it in a freezer until meteorologists could get there to measure it.

Eventually, of course, the record-breaking hailstone did melt, but not before the Coffeyville Convention and Visitors Bureau had the foresight to make a plaster cast replica, which now sits in a glass showcase near the front of the Dalton Defenders Museum.

To see the world-record-holding, rugby-ball-size hailstone, visit the museum at 113 East Eighth Street, just east of the downtown Plaza. Call (620) 251-5944.

Crime Doesn't Pay
Coffeyville

It's one of those unfortunate twists of fate. The Billy the Kids and the Son of Sams get all the glory. And their victims, the folks whose lives were cut short, are quickly relegated to the obit pages.

But not in Coffeyville. Here, the proud denizens celebrate the everyday Joes who, on October 5, 1892, stood up to the notorious

Dalton Gang when the gang brazenly rode into their own hometown to rob not one, but two banks, in the light of a sunny day. The would-be robbers got delayed by construction, giving every store clerk, farmer, teacher, and innocent bystander time to grab guns and put up a fight. Twelve minutes later, when all the smoke had cleared, eight men lay dead—four of the five Daltons and four defenders whose names are proudly remembered each year in the annual celebration that includes reenactments, pig kissing contests, an outhouse auction, and wheelbarrow races.

And, yes, the townsfolk still take care of their own. When a major industry pulled up stakes in 1998, leaving a 500,000-square-foot building empty and hundreds jobless, the city put together a proposal in two short weeks to lure Amazon.com to open what is now the bookseller's largest distribution center.

And as for the men who stood up to the Dalton Gang that October day, they were Lucius Baldwin, a dry goods store clerk; George Cubine, a shoemaker; Charles Connelly, the marshal; and Charles Brown, also a shoemaker.

Emmett Dalton, the youngest of the gang, survived, and was sentenced to life in the Kansas Penitentiary. He was pardoned by the governor after fourteen years and moved to California, where he wrote books and served as a consultant for the movie industry.

You can see the bullet holes left behind that day in the north brick wall in Death Alley. Visit www.coffeyville.com or call (800) 626-3357 to learn more about Dalton Defenders Days, which is always held the first full weekend of October.

Truth in Advertising
Elk Falls

Writers of travel brochures often exaggerate. When you show up to luxuriate in calm, serene waters, you find chlorine. When you look for the world's largest, you find second best. The Elk Falls travel brochure is nothing if not truthful.

★ ★

The writers of the brochure call it a living ghost town. For a small fee, they'll scrawl your name on a rock and drop it into a pothole. They'll even make you an honorary citizen. On one condition: that you promise not to move there. They're happy with their population of 101, thank you very much.

To find out more about this teensy tourist town that London's prized newspaper, *The Economist,* raved about, call Friends of Elk Falls at (620) 329-4425.

Out the Back and Down the Garden Path
Elk Falls

Every year the population of Elk Falls (101, according to my records) grows tenfold on the Friday and Saturday before Thanksgiving. Not because the town sells the world's most scrumptious turkeys (in fact, the closest grocery store is in Grenola, 14 miles away), but because it offers the most unusual "homes tour" available anywhere. I should probably call it the "part of a homes tour," because the only room shown is the backyard outhouse. Not that the town's outhouses are anything to sneeze at.

Every one of them is elaborately decorated and given a name. Postmaster Licia Nichols's entry on the Outhouse Tour (perchance the only working outhouse still used by the United States Postal Service?), for example, is called Postal Privy. There's an American flag, a gent built out of Priority boxes, and a story Licia wrote about "neither rain nor snow nor the postman needing to go."

Over the years, the tour has included the Gingerbread Outhouse (the seats on Hansel and Gretel's double-seater were painted red and white, like peppermint candy), a Chamber Pot (this elaborate porcelain throne was thrown by Steve Fry, the local potter), the Flower Pot (once a WPA outhouse, it was redesigned and sat next to the garden at the local B&B), the Nature Calls Outhouse (donated by the phone company, it had a phone receiver rather than a moon cut out on the door and included a little sign urging those who "have to go" to

★ ★

Über fire hydrant.
STEVE FRY

use the competitor's phone books first), and the Pooh Puppy Palace, designed around a fire hydrant. Everybody who comes to town for the festival and buys a button gets a map and a ballot for voting.

In 2008 *American Profile* magazine, well, profiled the outhouse tour and "outhouse enthusiasts came out of the woodwork," Fry says. "We got poems and songs and odes to the outhouse from thirty-five states."

★ ★

Most importantly, the article attracted the attention of Homer Allison, the country's foremost outhouse collector, who donated his entire collection to Elk Falls. So now, the local one-room schoolhouse has been transformed into the Homer Allison Outhouse Museum. Displays include electric corncobs, outhouse signs, and miniature out-houses made of everything from coal to copper.

For more information about the museum or the annual Elk Falls Outhouse Tour, call Friends of Elk Falls at (620) 329-4425.

I Would Have Moved to Kansas, Too
Elk Falls

Right outside Elk Falls is a historical marker erected by the State of Connecticut. While most states choose to erect historical markers within their own boundaries, Connecticut erected this one in Kansas to make up for a giant boo-boo it made in 1833.

Even though Connecticut sided with the Yankees in the Civil War, the state came out with a "Black Law" in 1833 to prevent black students from getting a free education. The law was passed after Prudence Crandall, an educator and human rights advocate, started New England's first academy for black females. For doing so, she was thrown in jail and endured three long court battles, all the while being harassed and hounded by local mobs. When the vigilantes started in on her students—throwing rocks through windows, setting the place on fire, and refusing to serve her students—she closed the school in order to protect them.

By the time Connecticut repealed the "Black Law" in 1838, Pru-dence had already moved to Illinois, where she continued the fight for equality and equal education for everyone.

So why is the historical marker in Kansas? In 1874, Prudence moved to Elk Falls with her brother, Hezekiah, to teach Native Americans.

In 1886 the Connecticut Legislature, supported by Mark Twain, apologized to Prudence, offered her a $400 monthly stipend, and even agreed to buy her old Connecticut home for her to retire in. She wisely "just said no." She died in Elk Falls on January 27, 1890.

More than a hundred years after her Connecticut trials, legal arguments used by her 1833 trial attorney were submitted to the Supreme Court during the historic civil rights case of Brown v. Topeka Board of Education. And in 1951 Walt Disney/NBC made a movie about Prudence's life, *She Stood Alone.*

The Connecticut marker is right next to the marker erected by the Kansas Historical Society on US 160 on the west edge of Elk Falls.

Cookies from Heaven
Emporia

Mr. Peanut, Bugs Bunny, Roy Rogers, and the Mona Lisa share a five-room house in Emporia.

Unlikely roommates, they do, thank goodness, have one thing in common. They're all cookie jars.

And they've all won a place in Charlotte Smith's Cookie Jar Heaven, a near 3,000 cookie jar collection that started almost twenty years ago while she was running the S&S

At last count, almost 3,000 cookie jars had died and gone to Cookie Jar Heaven.
MARY BETH HOWE-BERNHARDT

Cafe. To give the place a homey feel, Charlotte put up a shelf for her half dozen cookie jars. Before she knew it, customers started bringing in more cookie jars. Eventually, she had to buy a separate house to put them all in.

"I call it Cookie Jar Heaven because these cookie jars never have to work again," Smith says. Anybody who calls ahead can come and take a gander. But be prepared. It's doubtful you've ever seen so many shapes and sizes of cookie jars. Smith and her husband, John, who eventually joined her on the great cookie jar search, have cookie jars shaped like everybody from John Wayne to Smokey Bear to Mickey Mouse. They've got a whole shelf of cookie jars shaped like cars, and one that crows like a rooster when you take off its lid. They've even got cookie jars made to resemble their own relatives, Grandpa Washington and Grandma Bell.

Cookie Jar Heaven is at 121 Mechanic Street, but call (620) 343-3317 to set up a tour.

Not So National Dinosaur Monument
Erie

If you're still trembling from the *Jurassic Park* movies, don't even think about driving south of Erie on Highway 47. From a distance, you'll think you've accidentally stumbled into a time warp. Fifteen massive dinosaurs, some rearing their heads, others tending to their young, are grazing on Robert Dorris's property.

The retired Navy officer built the life-size dinosaurs out of scrap metal. And while they're certainly not real fossils, it would take an expert paleontologist to tell the difference. After studying each dinosaur, Dorris drew diagrams, took pictures of sculptures at museums, and began scouring through piles of scrap metal looking for discarded oil pans, pistons, crankshafts, and other pieces of metal that might make a vertebra or a skull. Among his collection of fifteen are *Velociraptors*, a *Pterodactyl*, a *Triceratops*, and a mom and baby *Eryops*.

Dorris's dinosaur fascination began after a visit to the Smithsonian back in the 1980s. Dorris says, "I was looking at the dinosaur skeletons at the Smithsonian and I thought, shoot, I could build one of these."

★ ★

Sure enough, he went home and made a *Brontosaurus* out of bolts, a gift he gave to his wife, Elveta. Next he made a *Teratosaurus* from welded car parts.

To visit the modern-day Jurassic Park, drive south of Erie on Highway 47.

If you build it, they will come.
GRASSROOTS ART CENTER

★ ★

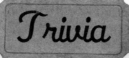

Trivia

More than 2,000 wild horses live in Greenwood County's tall grass pastures. The U.S. Bureau of Land Management pays $1.50 per day per horse, not bad dough. To qualify to babysit what the BLM calls "a natural resource," you gotta have 7¼ acres per wild horse.

Gravity of the Situation

Eureka

If you go to Colby College in Maine, Emory College in Atlanta, and eleven other college campuses across the eastern seaboard, you'll find monuments erected by the Gravity Research Foundation, a scientific clearinghouse that awards competitive grants to scientists conducting antigravity research. In return for planting these gravestone-resembling monuments, these thirteen small colleges received between $5,000 and $12,000 of stock (which eventually grew to millions of dollars) for gravity research. But in Eureka, the man who started the Gravity Research Foundation erected more than a monument. He built a whole college.

Roger Babson, a self-made millionaire, 1940 U.S. presidential candidate, and the first to predict the 1929 stock market crash, believed Eureka was the safest place in the United States to live. He called it the center of "The Magic Circle." He founded Utopia College there six years after his unsuccessful presidential bid.

A graduate of MIT and the author of forty-seven books, Babson became obsessed with gravity at the age of eighteen after his younger sister, Edith, drowned in Massachusetts's Annisquam River.

"She was unable to fight gravity," Babson later wrote, "which came up and seized her like a dragon and brought her to the bottom."

Unfortunately, the year after he opened Eureka's Utopia College, a second relative succumbed to the forces of gravity. Like Edith, his grandson drowned in New Hampshire's Lake Winnipesaukee. From that point until his death twenty years later, the eccentric Babson turned all efforts to the study of gravity, a force he believed could be conquered and controlled. Which could explain why Utopia College is now defunct.

But the building is still there, along with lots of beautiful Flint Hill scenery. If you'd like a personal tour from a one-man tourism dynamo, call Phil Johnston at (620) 583-6516. A former school-teacher and president of the Greenwood County Historical Society, Johnston does a monthly radio show on KOTE-FM (Coyote Radio) and, like Babson, believes Greenwood County "is one of the most beautiful spots on this good green earth."

Nanny Nanny Boo Boo
Fort Scott

Arlington National Cemetery might be more famous, but the National Cemetery in Fort Scott is older. Or at least that's what the sign on the edge of the cemetery says. It was the first of fourteen national cemeteries established by President Lincoln. Arlington, that also-ran, was number two. Buried here are sixteen Native American Civil War vets, black soldiers known as buffalo soldiers (their gravestones are shorter), and even some Confederate soldiers, but their graves are at an oblique angle. National Cemetery is located at 900 East National, (620) 223-2840.

Larger than Life
Fort Scott

Born in Fort Scott in 1912, Gordon Parks, the youngest of fifteen children, became a world-renowned photojournalist, filmmaker, novelist, poet, and composer. In 2004, Fort Scott Community College established the Gordon Parks Center for Culture and Diversity, and in

★ ★

October 2005 Parks himself donated $250,000 worth of photographs to the center. Before then, Parks's works in Fort Scott were displayed at Mercy Hospital.

Gordon Parks, who left Fort Scott when he was sixteen, bought a used camera in 1938—a camera that launched a preeminent career in photography (twenty years with *Life* magazine, to name one of his gigs) and film that included such movies as *Shaft, Leadbelly,* and a movie of his autobiographical novel, *The Learning Tree,* set, of course, in Kansas.

"Parks overcame a childhood filled with racism and poverty and chose to fight back with weapons of his own making—his mind, his creativity, and his art. He devoted his professional life to showing injustice and revealing beauty and in doing so made multiple substantive accomplishments to world culture and diversity," says Jill Walford, director of the center.

The Gordon Parks Center for Culture and Diversity is located at Fort Scott Community College, 2108 South Horton (800-874-3722, ext. 515).

Wish upon a Car
Galena

Lana Turner was discovered on a fountain stool at Schwab's drugstore. Natalie Portman was sitting in a pizza joint when an agent signed her to model. Tow Mater, the buck-toothed, redneck star of Disney's 2006 hit *Cars,* was discovered in a Kansas farm field with a tree growing through its middle. Pixar's Joe Ranfit spotted the rusted International Boom Truck that inspired the lovable Mater outside Galena while driving Route 66 for research. Today, the celebrity hunk of rusted metal sits at the north end of Galena's Main Street in front of a 1930s Kano-O-Tex gas station, fully restored. It even runs and, for the right price, will show up at parties.

The old gas station where Tow Mater poses daily with Route 66 travelers (13.2 miles of the Mother Road zooms right through Kansas) has been converted into a diner and gift shop that's stuffed to the rafters with Route 66 souvenirs and such *Cars* memorabilia as Tow Mater himself sculpted from clay. Called 4 Women on the Route, the diner is run by four Kansas friends who serve hearty road food (a specialty, of course, is Mater sandwiches: tomato, onion, and butter or mayo on white bread) and like to gab over the scrapbook they've put together of the gas station pre-restoration. As for the local celebrity (who has been renamed Tow Tater for obvious trademark reasons), his odometer reads 99,372 miles and his fuel tank resembles a beer keg. The diner is at 119 North Main Street, (620) 783-1366, www.4womenontheroute.com.

New York? Where's New York?
Girard

In 1922 the *Chicago Daily News* called Girard (population 2,722) the "Literary Capital of the United States." They knew what they were talking about. Two hugely successful publishing ventures were launched in this tiny burg in southeast Kansas.

The first, *Appeal to Reason,* a radical Socialist newspaper, was launched in 1897. By 1913 it was the largest-selling newspaper in the country, with a circulation of 750,000. Started by J. A. Wayland and masterminded by well-known liberal Fred Warren, who served as editor for ten years, the *Appeal* printed progressive articles advocating such radical ideas as the forty-hour workweek, the abolition of child labor, and pure food and drug laws.

All of the country's progressive thinkers wrote for the paper, including Jack London, Mary "Mother" Jones, Helen Keller, and Stephen Crane. In 1904, Warren paid little-known reporter Upton Sinclair $500 to write an investigative piece on the meat-packing industry in Chicago. The piece ran as seven weekly installments and was eventually bought by Doubleday, which published it as a book, *The Jungle.* By 1906 the book had become a huge best-seller and had been translated into twenty-seven languages.

★ ★

Constantly provoking controversy, the paper became a target for politicians and federal investigators. Warren was often thrown in jail, the paper's offices were broken into several times, and smear campaigns by such venerable competitors as the *Los Angeles Times* were waged on Wayland. On November 10, 1912, after newspaper leaks claimed he'd seduced an orphan who then died from the resulting abortion, Wayland committed suicide. His family, who continued to run the paper, eventually won libel suits against several newspapers, including the *L.A. Times.*

The final blow, however, came from J. Edgar Hoover and the Red Scare of 1919. In what's now known as the Palmer Raids, 10,000 Americans were rounded up and accused of supporting Communism. Many were shipped off to Russia. Subscribers got scared and canceled their subscriptions. The paper delivered its last issue on November 4, 1922.

The other publishing empire in Girard was Little Blue Books, a mail-order publishing company that sold small, inexpensive pamphlets of classic literature. Emanuel Haldeman-Julius, co-owner of *Appeal to Reason* after Wayland's death, had the dream of bringing literature to the common working man. He sold 3½-by-5-inch paperbacks of everything from Greek plays and the complete works of Shakespeare to *Alice's Adventures in Wonderland* and *Jam and Jelly-making for Beginners.*

Many of his 2,000 titles were reprints (H. G. Wells claimed he made much more money with Haldeman-Julius than with traditional publishers), but he also commissioned original works by such writers as family-planning pioneer Margaret Sanger, who wrote a Little Blue Book called *What Every Girl Should Know,* and Will Durant, who first published *The Story of Philosophy* with Haldeman-Julius.

Set in 8-point type and sold for a nickel, the books with the blue covers were a smash hit. More than 500 million were sold.

Once, while in New York, Haldeman-Julius was approached by two struggling publishers.

"Why," they wanted to know, "are you so successful there in

★ ★

backwater Kansas and we can't make it here in New York?"

Haldeman-Julius advised the men, who at that time were producing crossword puzzles, to publish a hardcover copy of Durant's *The Story of Philosophy*. Mr. Simon and Mr. Schuster took him up on his advice and the rest, shall we say, is history.

Often called "the Henry Ford of publishing," Haldeman-Julius made millions before he drowned in his backyard swimming pool. Little Blue Book fans included Emperor Haile Selassie of Ethiopia and Admiral Richard Byrd, who took a complete set on his expedition to the South Pole.

Although the Little Blue Printing Company burned to the ground in 1978, you can drive by the homes of Haldeman-Julius (east of Girard on Sinnet) and J. A. Wayland (721 North Summit Street). Back issues of *Appeal to Reason* and most of the 2,000 titles of Little Blue Books can be found in the special collections section of the Leonard H. Axe Library at Pittsburg State University, 1605 South Joplin Street, (620) 235-4879, www.library.pittstate.edu.

Hubbell's Rubble
Howard

In 1980, Jerry Hubbell signed up for a welding class at Independence Community College. It was a decision that can only be compared to Georgia O'Keeffe meeting Alfred Stieglitz.

"I thought I was taking it so I could work on my farm. You know, fix fences, keep the machines running," he says.

But before he knew it, he was using his welding torch to turn combine augers into mules and silo bottoms into 15-foot Wizard of Oz tin men.

His scrap metal creations, dubbed Hubbell's Rubble by the good folks of Howard, take up three city lots and create plenty of traffic. Visitors often stop by the WP outhouse that he hauled to the site to sign the guestbook.

"It's a two-seater. I call it my office," Jerry says. The guestbook has John Hancocks from pretty much every state in the union.

★ ★

"I still marvel and wonder how it really happened," says Jerry, who claims he never showed any inclination toward art before the welding class.

Soon after, though, his wife threw a dinner party for several of her gardening friends. As a joke, he welded together a female scarecrow on wheels, covered her with a sheet, tied some balloons to her, and unveiled her for the dinner party guests. He invited the six couples to come up with a name.

Tilly, the Tiller, she became. Soon she was joined by a dinosaur, Batman riding a motorcycle, a purple people eater, and a car named Maybelline.

"I just use stuff I find. Very rarely do I pay for anything," said Hubbell, who retired from welding in 2002 upon doctor's orders. Didn't complement his defibrillator, doc said.

To sign the guestbook in the outhouse office, visit Hubbell's Rubble on Highway 99, just inside the Howard city limits.

Just a Closer Walk with Thee
Humboldt

Humboldt's Biblesta is the largest parade in the world that depicts scenes from the Bible. Then again, it's probably the only parade in the world that depicts scenes from the Bible. Every float, every character, every band member has to be authentically dressed like Moses or Mary Magdalene or somebody else who graces the pages of the Good Book.

The Humboldt High School band usually starts the parade with the gospel classic, "Just a Closer Walk with Thee," then the floats, such as Jonah and a 40-foot whale that squirts water on the crowd, follow behind, circling the town square (if you can circle a town square).

Dr. Arthur Carlson Jr. is credited with hatching the unique parade theme back in 1957. While sitting at a prayer meeting, he suddenly remembered Apostle Paul's words that Christians should take their witness to the streets. The good Christians of Humboldt have been taking it to the streets ever since. (And speaking of streets, Humboldt has named many of its own after German philosophers. There's Schiller Street, Goethe Street, and Uhland Tritschlier Street, for example.)

Name a scene from the Bible and it has been featured at one time or another in the parade, which draws thousands from around the world to this little burg of 2,000. There have been floats featuring the Four Horsemen of the Apocalypse, the baptism of Jesus, and the Exodus, a walking float that always includes livestock. Gospel and contemporary Christian music are played on the town square, and a free bean supper begins promptly at 5 p.m.

The parade starts at 1 p.m., rain or shine, on the first Saturday in October. Amen.

People See, People Do
Independence

Independence, Kansas, played a pioneering role in America's space program. In 1959, a native of this southeast Kansas town was launched into space in a small capsule atop a Jupiter rocket. The pioneer astronaut, a monkey named Miss Able (there was also a Cain—get it?), survived her short trip of 300 miles at 10,000 mph, paving the way for human space travel.

Although she was not the first animal on a space mission, she was the first that actually lived to tell—er, rather, hoot—about it. Sadly, she died four days after her flight, as technicians tried to remove sensors from her heart. The upside is she made the cover of the June 15, 1959, issue of *Life* magazine.

To visit Miss Able's chimphood home, visit Ralph Mitchell Zoo's Monkey Island at Riverside Park in Independence. The 124-acre park also has a unique kiddy playland with concrete dinosaurs and nursery rhyme characters, a carousel that still costs five cents, a miniature train ride that will set you back a mere quarter, and a miniature golf course that tells the history of Independence in eighteen holes.

Riverside Park is located at the corner of Penn Avenue and Oak Street. For more information visit www.forpaz.com.

The List Goes On

Also in Independence:

- Shulthis Stadium, the first stadium in the country where baseball was played under lights. The game was April 28, 1930. The Independence Yankees, a farm team for the bigs, built the stadium and then, nineteen years later, hired a little-known player named Mickey Mantle, who played his first season there in 1949. The stadium is in Riverside Park.

- The most comprehensive collection of native son William Inge's work. The Pulitzer prize–winning author wrote *Picnic, Bus Stop,* and the Academy Award–winner *Splendor in the Grass,* to name a few.

- Lots of big historic mansions. In 1901 and 1902, Independence had more millionaires per capita than any city in the country. The millions were made from three things that were discovered in Independence: natural gas, oil, and limestone, which was used to make concrete.

Off Their Rocker
LeRoy

Okay, so I'm not going to try to pull a fast one on you. The giant rocking chair in LeRoy isn't the world's largest. There's one in Hattiesburg, Mississippi, that's 30 feet tall, one in Lippan, Texas, that's 26 feet, and one in Penrose, Colorado, that stacks up at 21 feet. But LeRoy's behemoth rocker is the only one of the four-rocker set that fronts a jerky smokehouse and the only one that has an accompany-ing 1920 manure spreader attached to biplane wings. Let's just say, all four of the big rockers would be hard for the average granny to mount.

The LeRoy Rocker was built in Eureka Springs, Arkansas, for Mar-tin Luther, the former slaughterhouse manager who runs Luther's Smokehouse and Luther's Jerky. Since the rocker's nearly impossible for anyone but NBA centers to enjoy, Luther is kind enough to offer a rocking booth inside the restaurant/convenience store where his smoked meats are offered up with all the fixings. The jerky, which Luther and his eight employees mail order around the world, comes in liver, beef, pork, buffalo, ham, turkey, teriyaki, jalapeño, and pem-mican. All varieties come with Luther's "Dog Ate It" guarantee. But as he says, you can't blame the dog if the mailman leaves something this delectable on the front porch.

Luther's Jerky is on 98 Sixth Street, (800) 322-0868, www.jerky usa.com.

36-24-36. NOT
Madison

Necessity is the mother of invention. Plato coined the term. Janet Fish, an artist from Madison, is Exhibit A. She became a doll artist in 1982 because her son begged for an E.T. doll. The popular movie had just come out and, as a mother of four, she couldn't afford the $20 it took to buy her insistent child a store-bought extraterrestrial.

"I took a leg from a pair of stockings, glued on a couple eyes, and he didn't know the difference. He carried it everywhere," she explains the impetus for her nearly thirty-year career as a doll artist.

Her creations have morphed over the years. After E.T., she turned to porcelain dolls, even taught classes for a spell.

"That was fun, but it finally occurred to me that I was making the same doll over and over," she says. "I wasn't letting my imagination take over."

That's certainly not the case today. Fish's dolls, which regularly show up in galleries and collections across the country, are anything but clones. Each is a unique creation, made of cloth or polymer clay or feathers or premade body parts rearranged in a way that, let's just say, Mattel would never approve. A recent doll, for example, was made from a leg. It had wings, a head on the thigh, and two left feet.

"I may call her the Monarch of the Flint Hills," Fish says.

Besides doll making, the avid artist draws and paints. In fact, after her 2006 knee surgery, she found that the answer to the question, "How do you spell relief?" was c-o-l-o-r-e-d- p-e-n-c-i-l-s.

"I was in a lot of pain and drawing was the only thing that could stop it. I was so deep into the right brain that the pain receded into nothingness," she explains. "I drew every day and it provided relief."

Fish's whole house on the edge of Madison serves as her studio, a fact not lost on her husband.

"He seems to like having all these body parts lying around," she says.

Her largest doll, a life-size specimen that sits in a chair besides the staircase by the front window, has startled more than one workman.

"They always pretend that they don't jump, but they do," she says.

To see Janet's dolls, check out her Web site at www.madtel .net/~fishbowl/.

But, Captain, I Don't See an Ocean
Neodesha

In the tiny one-stoplight town of Neodesha, 1,500 miles from the nearest ocean, there's a factory with a big sign: THROUGH THESE DOORS WALK THE FINEST BOAT BUILDERS IN THE WORLD. Indeed, Cobalt's 300 to 400 boat builders, mostly farmers, make luxury sport boats, 20- to 29-foot runabouts, with the best reputation in the industry.

When Pack St. Clair, owner of the family-run business that also sells yachts, built his first Cobalt in 1968, he drove it out to California for a boat show. A then-outsider, he was refused admittance, but since he'd poured his last dime into building the boat, he figured he might as well stick around. He parked it in a gas station across from the boat show where everybody could see it. Sure enough, a San Ramon, California, dealer took one look at his boat's sleek lines and ingenious flowing power hump and signed on to be the first dealer. Today, the company has one hundred dealers across the globe, makes 2,600 boats and $125 million per year, and happily gives tours to anyone who shows up at the factory in Neodesha.

"We know from experience that once a customer sees what we do here, realizes the work ethic involved, we've got 'em for life," says Alex Barry, regional manager of Western United States.

Call ahead and they'll take you on a tour at 1715 North Eighth Street, (800) 468-5764, www.cobaltboats.com.

Abbie Hoffman, You Weren't the First
Pittsburg

The world's first protest march occurred in southeast Kansas. It was December 1921 when nearly 6,000 women, wearing ragged coats and carrying their babies, marched to protest management's decision to replace their coal-mining husbands with scabs, most of them fraternity boys from local colleges. In those days, there were 517 mines in southeast Kansas; the miners, who often worked lying on their sides, were lucky to make $1.25 a day. Conditions were wretched, pay was arbitrarily withheld, and more than 200 miners in Crawford and Cherokee Counties were injured or killed in 1921 alone.

The protesters, wives of the miners who were already striking, got mad. They blocked the entrances to the mines with American flags, beat on the bosses with brooms, and sang songs of solidarity in French, Slovene, German, and Italian. The panicked governor of Kansas set up a command post at Pittsburg's Stilwell Hotel, and the state militia, including a machine gun company, was activated.

The nation had never seen anything like it. "Near-anarchy" said the *New York Times,* which dubbed the women "The Amazon Army." The press raced to southeast Kansas from around the world.

By the end of December, forty-nine of the women had been arrested and jailed, shots had been fired, and the local union had sent its miners back to work. The Kansas coal industry began its long slide into oblivion, and the Amazon Army was largely forgotten.

Thanks to Lawrence artist Wayne Wildcat, who is part Yuchi Indian, a 10-by-12-foot mural of the march was recently unveiled. You can see it at the Pittsburg Public Library, Fourth and Walnut Streets, (620) 231-8110, www.pittsburgpubliclibrary.org.

Communes in Kansas

In Bourbon County, you'll find Vegetarian Creek, named for a former Kansas commune. The Vegetarian Settlement Company bought sixteen square miles of farmland in the Kansas territory in 1862. The ambitious company, which originated in New York, planned an octagonal community with 102 wedge-shaped farms of sixteen acres each. Many vegetable-loving settlers bought shares in the company, which promised an eventual hydropathic estate, an agricultural college, a scientific institute, and a museum of curiosities to go along with the farmland. Although the company had good intentions, most of what they promised never materialized. Miriam Davis Colt, one of the shareholders who traveled from New York to Kansas, published a diary of her life at the commune. It was called *I Went to Kansas: A Thrilling Account of an Ill-Fated Expedition to Fairy Land.*

★ ★

Whole Lotta Cluckin' Going On
Pittsburg

Not 100 yards from each other in a virtual ghost town are not one but two wildly successful fried-chicken restaurants that together seat more than 800 people. What's more, they've been wildly successful for more than six decades.

Chicken Annie (aka Ann Frances Rehak Pichler) and Chicken Mary (Mary Zerngast) both started frying chicken in their homes when their coal-mining hubbies lost their jobs. Annie's husband, Charles, lost his leg in March 1933 while sitting on a railroad coal car. Because the coal mining companies could no longer use an amputee, Annie, with three small children at home, was forced to think quick. She opened her three-room home to her husband's former coworkers, who gladly paid her 15 cents for a mug of home brew and a ham or veal sandwich. Before long, the Pichlers had to add more rooms and more items to the menu. By 1934, Annie was serving three pieces of fried chicken, German potato salad, German coleslaw with garlic, green peppers, a tomato slice, and bread for a whopping 75 cents.

In 1941, Chicken Mary, who lived across the street, had a similar string of bad luck when her husband, Joe, came down with a strange illness that caused him to lose his job. She too opened her kitchen table and began attracting coal miners, who would knock on the door anytime, night or day, to hustle a meal. Within four years, she and Joe moved a pool hall they picked up cheap from a nearby mining camp to the lot next door. Although they originally called their pool-hall-turned-restaurant Joe's Place, it soon became known far and wide as Chicken Mary's because Mary, who was 5-foot-1 and just about as wide, was a real character who pinned her apron on with two safety pins.

Today the mining camps are closed and the restaurants are run by the Chicken ladies' kids and grandkids. Located 5 miles north of Fourth Street and Broadway on US 69 and 3 miles east on US 160, both are open 4 to 8:30 p.m. Tuesday through Friday, 4 to 9 p.m. Saturday, and 11 a.m. to 8 p.m. Sunday. Chicken Annie's, (620) 231-9460; Chicken Mary's, (620) 231-9510.

Bet You Didn't Know They Were from Kansas

- **Dennis "The Menace" Mitchell.** In Hank Ketcham's 1990 auto-biography, he explained that five-year-old Dennis, his patient parents Henry and Alice Mitchell, dog Ruff, and cat Hot Dog actually live in Wichita. Henry works at a local aeronautical engineering company and George Wilson, the grouchy neighbor, is retired from the post office. The naughty but lovable Kansan has appeared in at least two movies, a television series, and a daily comic strip that is still run in 1,000 newspapers in forty-eight countries.

- **Superman.** Like Dennis, Superman grew up "secretly" in Kansas. In a 1986 Man of Steel comic book, the superhero made the comment, "At heart, I'm just a boy from a small town in Kansas." Before that announcement, readers just knew he was from "Smallville," somewhere in the heart of America. Producers of Christopher Reeve's 1978 film filled the screen with wide-open fields of waving wheat, grain elevators, and even a Kansas Star passenger train to be outrun by the teenage orphan from planet Krypton. In ABC's *Lois and Clark,* the crime-fighting investigative reporter often flew home to Kansas to visit his Smallville parents.

- **The Birdman of Alcatraz.** Although he's known for his stint at the Alcatraz penitentiary in San Francisco, Robert Stroud, the "Birdman of Alcatraz," spent more than thirty years in the federal penitentiary in Leavenworth, Kansas. Transferred there in 1912, he received extension diplomas from Kansas State University in mechanical drawing, engineering, mathematics, music, and theology. In 1920 he began studying birds and was soon publishing articles and books about birds and their diseases.

- **Olive Oyl.** Marilyn Schreffler, who did the voice for Popeye the

Sailor's cartoon girlfriend, was born in Wichita, graduated from Topeka West, and attended Topeka's Washburn University. Besides being Olive Oyl, Schreffler has appeared in numerous TV commercials, including some for Alka-Seltzer and Dole pineapple.

- **Mary Ann.** You're a true trivia expert if you know Mary Ann's character in *Gilligan's Island* used to work at a department store in Winfield, Kansas.

- **Smokey Bear.** Artist Rudolph Wendelin first drew Smokey (this was before he was a real bear) in Atwood, Kansas.

- **The first husband of the Duchess of Windsor.** Earl Winfield Spencer Jr., who was married to Wallis Simpson before she married the dethroned king of England, was born in Kinsley, Kansas.

- **The creator of Geech.** Jerry Bittle, creator of the popular syndicated comic strip, got his first job as a professional artist at his hometown newspaper, the *Wichita Eagle-Beacon.* In the early 1980s, he created Geech, a comic strip based on his memories of Kansas. Artie, a regular character in the strip, sometimes wears a sweatshirt from Bittle's alma mater, Wichita State University.

- **Dennis Hopper.** It was cowboy movies at the Saturday matinees in Dodge City that first inspired Dennis Hopper to take up acting. He was born in Dodge City and grew up on his grandparents' farm nearby while his father was away in the military.

- **The creator of Porky Pig.** Melvin "Tubby" Millar was often found by his family in Portis, Kansas, doodling cartoons on the side of his homework. His talent took him to Hollywood and a job with Warner Brothers, where he created many Looney Tunes characters, most notably Porky Pig.

- **Buster Keaton.** His Kansas birth was a bit of an accident. As acrobats, his parents were appearing in a traveling tent show with magician Harry Houdini. While spending the night in Piqua, a windstorm blew down their tent; their son Joseph (he didn't earn the

(Continued on next page)

(Continued from previous page.)

name Buster until he was a toddler) was born a few hours later in the church where they took shelter. The star of more than one hundred silent movies returned to his birthplace only once, when he drove through town in his chauffeur-driven limousine.

- **Emmett Kelly.** The famous circus clown was born in Sedan and lived there until his father quit his job with the railroad and bought a farm in Missouri.

- **Vivian Vance.** Born Vivian Jones in Cherryvale, this actress who had to agree to wear frumpy clothes and be ten to twenty pounds overweight in her most notorious role as Lucille Ball's sidekick, moved to Independence when she was two. Her parents opened a grocery store there.

- **The scarecrow in *The Wizard of Oz.*** The actor Fred Stone, who played the Scarecrow on Broadway, lived in a string of Kansas towns with his father, a traveling barber. His first performance was as a tightrope walker in Topeka when he was eleven.

- **The actor who played Charlie Chan.** Sidney Toler, who made twenty-two appearances as the clever Chan, was raised in Kansas. His parents owned a grocery store in Anthony in south central Kansas.

- **Erin Brockovich.** The real Erin Brockovich was born and raised in Lawrence, Kansas. Her parents still live there.

- **Hugh Beaumont.** Dad to Wally and "The Beav," Beaumont's Ward Cleaver was also born in Lawrence. When he was in high school his family moved to California, where he was discovered in a Hollywood talent search. After retiring from acting, he moved back to the Midwest (Minnesota) to raise Christmas trees.

Between a Rock and a Hard Place
Sedan

Nobody knows for sure who built England's megalithic ruin known as Stonehenge. Some claim it was the Druids. Others say Merlin himself conjured up the ancient rock formation.

Thanks to the conveniences of modern civilization, we will never need to question the genesis of Prairiehenge, the half-acre earthwork that overlooks a valley just west of Sedan. Barring some unforeseen disaster, we will always know that this tribute to the tallgrass prairie and the Osage Indians was built by artist Stan Herd, who spent a year forming the thirteen-ton limestone rocks into two overlapping circles.

Commissioned by A&E personality Bill Kurtis, who owns the 10,000-acre ranch where it rests, Prairiehenge was strategically designed in what Kurtis calls "the secret meadow" of his Red Buffalo Ranch. He bought the ranch, near his boyhood home, soon after 9/11, to get back in touch with the land. "When towers fall, you reach out for some permanent anchor," he says. "Here you can feel the pulse of earth beneath your feet."

At last count, Kurtis was grazing 1,000 head of cattle and fifty buffalo on his ranch.

Although groups can make arrangements to visit Prairiehenge, the blackjack oak grove where Prairiehenge rests is not officially open to the public. To find out more, contact Kurtis's Red Buffalo Gift Shop, 107 East Main, (620) 725-4022, http://theredbuffalo.com.

Who Needs a Concert Hall?
Strong City

The Lincoln Center for the Performing Arts probably has pretty good acoustics. I know it has lots of cushy seats, fancy bathrooms, and a lobby with tapered columns of travertine. But I'd pit the concert hall for the inaugural Symphony in the Flint Hills against New York's any day.

The backdrop for the Kansas symphony: green rolling hills, circling hawks, and the infinite sky of the Tallgrass National Preserve near Cottonwood Falls. An eighty-five-piece orchestra accompanied by a one-hundred-voice chorus playing outdoors in the middle of one of the last stands of tallgrass prairie left in the United States.

The inspiration for the Symphony in the Flint Hills was a birthday party for rancher Jane Koger, who celebrated her fortieth in 1994 with a sixty-piece all-woman orchestra. More than 3,000 folks from Kansas, the Midwest, and beyond set up lawn chairs and sprawled on blankets to witness the outdoor symphony concert on her Homestead Ranch, a 4,000-acre cattle ranch near Matfield Green that year. Ever since that magical night, people had been asking, "When can we do it again?"

The Symphony in the Flint Hills answered that question by establishing an annual event held at changing outdoor venues on the tallgrass prairies of the Flint Hills. For more information, contact Symphony in the Flint Hills, Inc. at 311 Cottonwood Avenue, P.O. Box 441, Strong City, KS 66869 (620-273-8955; www.symphonyinthe flinthills.org).

Ma, Pa, Laura, and Mary Were Here
Wayside

Of Laura Ingalls Wilder's nine books, *Little House on the Prairie* remains the most popular, having spawned a popular TV series and sold some five million copies since it was published in 1935. The "little house" Wilder wrote about (if it were still standing) would be in Wayside (if it were still a town). Lucky for true Little House–philes, the little house, which was really more like a 14-by-16-foot log cabin, has been authentically re-created in the very spot where it once stood. There's also a well that Pa and Mr. Scott dug; Sunny Side school, an 1871 schoolhouse where Laura would have gone had she been old enough; and a post office where she might have sent a letter had she known how to write back then.

When the log cabin was erected by Pa Ingalls in 1870, it was the eighty-ninth residence in Rutland Township. Laura lived there from 1870 until 1871, when her family learned that they'd mistakenly built the durn thing on property belonging to the Osage Indian Reservation. They moved back to Wisconsin, never knowing that six months later the land was opened to homesteaders and, therefore, they could have stayed.

To see the cabin that looks an awful lot like the one Michael Landon and Melissa Gilbert hung out in, visit the Little House that sits 13 miles southwest of Independence off Highway 75. Call (620) 289-4238 or visit www.littlehouseontheprairie.com for more information.

The Big Dipper
West Mineral

In its heyday, Big Brutus, a sixteen-story coal shovel, could lift out enough coal to fill three railroad cars with every scoop. But that was to be expected of a monster machine that weighed 135 tons, took a year to assemble, and required three men just to operate it. Twenty-four hours a day it ran, working hard for the Pittsburg and Midway Coal Mining company, which paid $6.5 million to have it built and hired 150 railroad cars to bring it to southeast Kansas from Ohio.

But by 1974, coal prices dropped to $5 a ton. It cost $12 a ton just to use Big Brutus (the crazy thing used enough electricity to power a city with a population of 15,000), so the big cheese at the Pittsburg and Midway made a savvy business decision: Better shut the old shovel down. They tried to pawn it off on interested buyers, asking $5 million, but nobody even made an offer. It was too big to move (even disassembling it would cost a small fortune), so the company eventually donated it to a nonprofit in West Mineral, offering to paint it black and orange, company colors, for free.

Today it's a popular tourist attraction, drawing 30,000 visitors a year. Brooke Shields was one of those 30,000, and you can see her autograph ("To the miners. Love and kisses, Brooke Shields") in the visitor center. The visitor center also has old mining drills, historical pictures, and Little Giant, the world's smallest working replica of an electric mining shovel. Little Giant was built by a hobbyist back in the 1930s. It took him eleven years to finish, not too hard to believe when you realize it has 30,000 rivets and 2,000 bolts. The visitor center also offers yo-yos, Frisbees, playing cards, and even Christmas ornaments with pictures of Big Brutus.

Guests willing to fork over $8 can make the breathtaking climb to the top. One couple even exchanged wedding vows up there.

Dig this. In its heyday Big Brutus could fill three railroad cars in a single scoop.

★ ★

You can't really miss a 160-foot orange and black coal shovel, but its exact location is 6 miles west of the K-7 and K-102 junction, then ¼ mile south. Call (620) 827-6177; www.bigbrutus.org.

Cows in Space

In 1897, the Yates Center newspaper reported that Alexander Hamilton had come out of his house one afternoon to discover a cigar-shaped UFO hovering over his farm. According to the article, spacemen from the ship had roped one of Hamilton's calves and were trying to hoist it on board.

The article had verification from Yates Center's leading citizens, who vouched for the veracity of Hamilton's claims. For nearly one hundred years, it was considered one of the best-documented UFO cases on the books. But there was just one problem. It was all a big hoax.

It seems Hamilton, along with his vouchers, belonged to the local liar's club. Once a week, they got together and attempted to outdo each other with tall tales. Hamilton's calfnapping story was so good that the paper published it as a joke. Little did they know that thousands of people around the world would be dumb enough to believe it. It wasn't until 1977 that Jerry Clark of *FATE* magazine published the real truth.

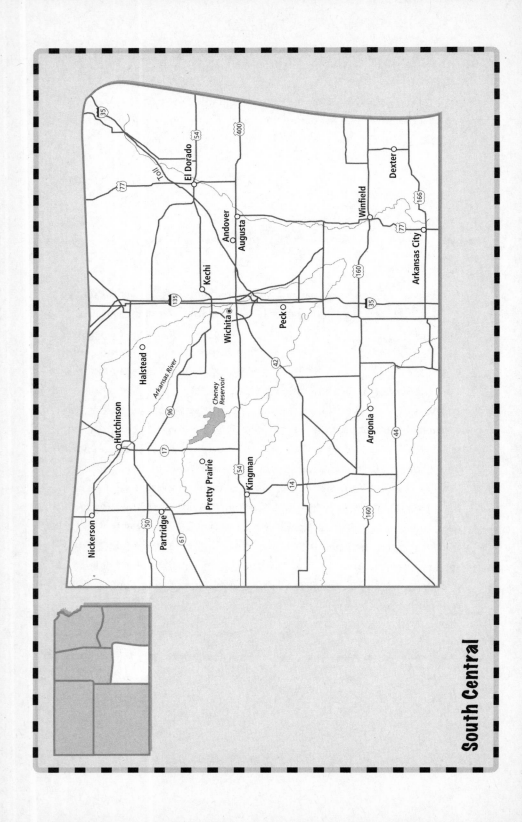

South Central

4

South Central

As hard as I try, I just can't rein in the superlatives when talking about south central Kansas. There are just too many world's largests and world's firsts in this part of the state to remain humble.

For starters, the world's largest collection of space suits and the world's largest piece of salt can be found in one south central town.

And if that wasn't enough, the world's first female mayor was elected in Argonia and the world's first Pizza Hut was established in Wichita.

So if you notice a tendency to brag, forgive me.

Of course, I prefer to call it editorial honesty. When I say South Central Kansas is one of the best places in the world to buy elderberry wine, I'm not exaggerating. When I drop names like Albert Einstein (whose brain lived on in Kansas long after his death), Frederic Remington (who got his artistic inspiration on a sheep farm in south central Kansas), and Peter the Great (his very own autograph resides in Wichita), I'm not pulling a fast one. Basically, I'm telling it like it is. South Central Kansas is one heck of a place.

★ ★

Rocket Men
Argonia

Turns out, NASA isn't the only organization launching rockets. K.L.O.U.D Busters, a group of Kansas rocket enthusiasts, launch high-powered rockets that regularly break the sound barrier. In fact, their forty-acre "rocket pasture" outside Argonia has been approved to launch rockets up to 50,000 feet. Of course, you have to get an FAA-approved waiver if you're going higher than 25,000 feet. Five times, the Kansas pasture has been chosen to host the prestigious national Tripoli Rocketry Association's L.D.R.S., which any rocket scientist worth his boosters can tell you stands for *Large and Dangerous Rocket Ships.*

At least once a month, the one hundred-plus members get together to fly their home-built rockets, many taller than them, with engines creating 16,000 pounds of thrust and reaching Mach 1 speeds. Not all rockets are as tall as Paul Bunyan. Experimental rockets are sometimes fashioned out of Legos or old footballs. With a state-of-the-art launch pad that can lift up to sixty-four rockets simultaneously, the club regularly hosts rocket drag races. There's a public address system, a tent for spectators, and FM broadcasts of the launch control officer's countdowns and play-by-plays.

K.L.O.U.D., in case you're wondering, stands for *Kansas Lower Orbital Unmanned Delegation.* AirFest, an annual four-day event held every Labor Day, promises ground-shaking, flame-shooting fun.

The rocket pasture is located on Highway 44, 7 miles south of Argonia, 1 mile east of Argonia Road. Contact them at K.L.O.U.D Busters, Inc. c/o Science Education Center, 2730 Boulevard Plaza, Wichita, KS 67211-3812, www.kloudbusters.org.

Guess That Nomination Backfired
Argonia

The first woman mayor was elected in Kansas in 1887, thirty-three years before women nationally received the right to vote. Town drunks thought it would be funny to put the name of Susanna Salter,

★ ★

head of Argonia's Temperance Committee, on the ballot for mayor. Unbeknownst to her, Salter was elected by two thirds of Argonia's voters. It turned out to be a joke that backfired on her nominating committee: The first thing Salter did was ban the sale of alcohol and close the town's bars.

Other Kansas women have gone on to be "firsts," including Amelia Earhart, Rena Milner (the first woman city manager), Mabel Chase (the first woman county sheriff), Julia Archibald Holmes (the first woman to climb Pike's Peak), Lucy Hobbs Taylor (the first woman dentist), Georgia Neese Clark Gray (the first woman U.S. treasurer), and Minnie Morgan (the first to head an all-female city government).

To see the brick home that Susanna Salter lived in when she reigned as the country's first female mayor, visit 220 West Garfield Street in Argonia. Even though she never ran for office again and eventually moved to Oklahoma (where she died in 1961 at the age of 101), her Argonia home is on the National Register of Historic Places and operates as a museum. To arrange a tour, call Mary Beth Bookless at (620) 435-6171.

Sing a Song of Six Pens
Arkansas City

Most Kansas farms raise cattle, pigs, or wheat. Bill Post's family farmstead raises voices, in beautiful harmonic song.

The hen house, for example, rather than sheltering real hens and real eggs, has fiberglass ones. When you walk in the door and push a button, Bill Post's song "The Old Red Rooster and His Flock of Red Hens" starts playing.

Likewise, the century-old granary shelters Old Jack, a fiberglass mule. Push that building's button and you get Post's hit "The Old Gray Mules."

The Post Musical Homestead, as it's called, was homesteaded in 1874 by Harvey T. Post. When Harvey's grandson, Bill Post, and his wife, Orvaleen, were trying to decide what to do with the family farm, they made the logical choice. They decided to turn it into a museum of Bill's illustrious six-decade career in the music business.

Bill wrote what could be the theme song for this book, "Where in the World but Kansas?" He has six albums and more than one hundred songs under his musical writing belt.

Post and his first wife, Doree (she died in 1951), wrote songs for, among others, Lawrence Welk, Connie Stevens ("Sixteen Reasons" has sold more than two million copies), and the Lettermen. The prolific singing/songwriting team also cut six of their own albums, including their first demo, which was recorded in the garage of Les Paul, the guy who invented the electric guitar.

Tin Pan Alley, another of the farm's five buildings, showcases Bill and Doree's many albums and records with labels such as MGM, RCA Victor, Capitol Records, and Rainbow Records.

The Post Musical Homestead is officially open once a year, but if you call (620) 442-4336 and ask nicely, Bill or his son John may give you a personal tour. Take US 166 out of Ark City.

Sixty-three Careers and Counting
Arkansas City

If you go to Canon City, Colorado, you'll find a tourist attraction called Buckskin Joe's. It's probably a fine establishment, probably has lots of Wild West tomfoolery. But I have a problem with it because the real Buckskin Joe, the one who could play sixteen musical instruments, turn somersaults over the backs of horses, and hit small objects with a bow and arrow, was actually from Arkansas City, Kansas.

I can't make the argument that he never left Ark City. He made numerous expeditions into the silver fields of Colorado, the wilds of Honduras, and the depths of Nova Scotia, but his home base for all of these adventures was none other than Arkansas City, Kansas.

Edward Jonathan Hoyt (aka Buckskin Joe) was one of the first to

Trivia

Famed actress Elizabeth Taylor celebrated her first Christmas in Arkansas City, where both her maternal grandfather and grandmother (for whom she was named) lived. She also attended Ark City's Roosevelt Elementary when she was nine.

homestead the area now known as Arkansas City. He built a home there, owned a grocery store there. Customers often had to wait on themselves, because Buckskin Joe and his partner were usually turning flips in the gymnasium they built in the back.

He served as U.S. Marshal for the newly opened Oklahoma territory, led expeditions into Indian country, and ran a beekeeping operation, all from Ark City.

For fun, he strung a wire from the town's two tallest buildings and walked the tightrope. One summer, when crowds of kids gathered, he pushed a wheelbarrow across the tightrope, stopping in the center to start a fire. After his third daughter, Belle, was born, he offered to take her across the wire with him. His wife wisely refused.

From Ark City, he formed the Cow Horn Band, the Ragged Ass Militia (so named because many of its members fought in tattered overalls and underwear), and his very own Buckskin Joe's Wild West Shows that had bronc riders, bucking horses, wild steers, and a bona fide "Pete-haw-e-rat" Indian village.

To find out more about Buckskin Joe, visit the Cherokee Strip Museum, located 1.6 miles south of the intersection of US 166 and US 77. Phone (620) 442-6750.

Dr. Jensen and Mr. Henry
Augusta

Franklin Jensen, a mild-mannered former high school English teacher with a quick sense of humor, just can't seem to keep Huntington David Troll away from his twenty-eight-acre farm east of Augusta. Henry, as the troll is nicknamed, keeps making these elaborate metal sculptures out of old farm machinery. There's a 20-foot praying mantis, a grasshopper as big as a truck, a lion, and a boy walking a cow home from the pasture.

Maybe Jensen lets the persnickety Henry keep working because he also creates scenes from Jensen's favorite literature: one from "Chanson Innocente," by e.e. cummings, featuring Pan and four children, and another of Don Quixote charging a replica of a sixteenth-century Spanish windmill, for example.

If you stop by Highway 400 to see the work, Jensen could be there passing out a printed story about the artist, Henry, a misanthropic hermit who has mysteriously never been seen by human eyes.

Jensen, who grew up on a farm, began his artistic career in 1978 after taking a welding class. He started with furniture and outdoor wall hangings fashioned from scrap iron. Outside his home are hanging portraits of Abe Lincoln, Henry David Thoreau, Mark Twain, and Ben Franklin. For several years, his Jensen's Oak and Iron was a popular business in Wichita.

Twenty years ago, tired of cramped urban quarters, he bought the acreage outside Augusta. That's when he started making the spectacular freestanding sculptures, many of which can be seen from Highway 400.

The first thing you'll notice is Redbone, a running bison made from strips of redwood decking. Henry's Sculpture Hills, as the area is known, is located 4 miles east of Augusta. If you want to meet Henry, all I can say is, "Good luck." Call (316) 775-5296 or visit www.sculpturehill.com for more information.

★ ★

The Other O. Henry
Dexter

Groundskeepers at Wrigley Field were more than relieved when out-fielder Henry Rodriquez was traded to the Florida Marlins. After all, they're the ones that had to clean up all the Oh Henry! wrappers. Every time the popular slugger hit a homerun, the fans celebrated by throwing wrappers onto the field. But, interestingly enough, the popular candy bar, which is claimed by a Chicago candy company, was actually invented in Kansas. Only then, it was called the Tom Henry, after the candy maker who invented it. Henry, who was trained by a Greek candy maker in Boston, traveled the country as a candy troubleshooter. If you had problems with your horehound, for example, you'd hire Tom Henry to work out the bugs. While working for Ranney-Davis in Ark City, he invented a caramel peanut fudge bar dipped in chocolate. The year was 1919 and the bar was an immediate hit. When he sold it to the Curtiss Candy Company a few years later, the name was changed to Oh Henry! By the time Nestle bought it, the candy bar already had such a strong following that no one even considered changing its name.

After Ranney-Davis went belly up during the Depression, Tom Henry moved to Little Rock, Arkansas, where he opened his own place, the Better Mousetrap Candy Shop. The Better Mousetrap—pecans and almonds dipped in a chocolate cup—and several other Tom Henry recipes are still being made at Henry's Candy Store in Dexter. Tom Henry's son, Patrick, moved to Dexter and started his own candy store in the mid-1950s. His daughter, Evelyn Pudden, and her two daughters now run the factory. They make one hundred kinds of candy, producing some 70,000 pounds a year.

And yes, they still make the Oh Henry! Only they call it the Momma Henry.

Henry's Candy is open seven days a week from 8 a.m. (9 a.m. on Sunday) to 5 p.m. Call (620) 876-5423 for more information.

First Thing You Know, Ol' Jed's a Millionaire . . .
El Dorado

In 1918, the oil fields of El Dorado produced 10 percent of the world's oil. Many lucky ranchers who leased their land to Cities Service became overnight millionaires. Oil wells were being dug at the rate of 3½ per day.

Oil Hill, a company town with 2,500 people, was the largest town in the world without so much as a shred of municipal government. It didn't need one. The company built swimming pools, golf courses, schools, gyms, stores, and post offices for their many employees who unloaded trainloads of pipes, erected wood and steel derricks, and managed machine shops that kept the oil wells going. The El Dorado oil field covered 34 square miles and contained 1,800 producing oil wells.

By 1957, Oil Hill, like other lease towns in Butler County, was gone. All that remains today are sidewalks, abandoned flower beds, a company garage, and a Quonset hut.

But never fear, the history of black gold, Texas tea is available at El Dorado's Kansas Oil Museum, just 2 blocks from downtown. You can't miss the 100-foot steel oil derrick (it still works) and the ten acres of historic oil field equipment. It's open daily at 383 East Central Avenue (316-321-9333; www.kansasoilmuseum.org).

She Says That's Her Gall Bladder, but I Can See Right through Her
Halstead

She's almost fifty, but doesn't look a day over twenty-eight. Valeda III, the life-size transparent talking woman of the Kansas Learning Center for Health in Halstead, has taught thousands of Kansas kids how their veins and arteries work. She has shown them her own nerves, her own heart, and her own lymphatic system, all of which light up when she mentions them in her fifteen-minute presentation on "how the body works."

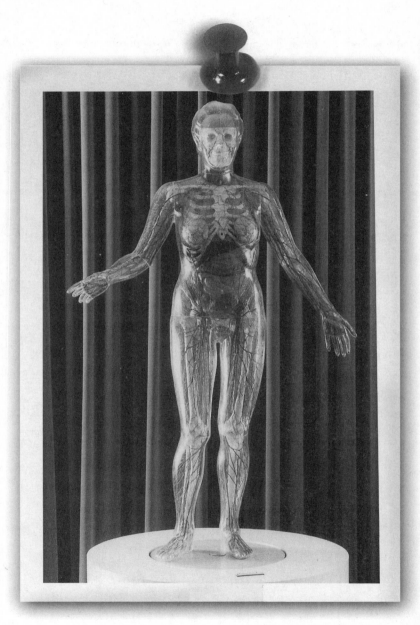

Valeda has nothing to hide.
KANSAS LEARNING CENTER FOR HEALTH

★ ★

Trivia

Job Diner, a tiny diner that shares a building with Hot Rod Bail Bonding, has fourteen red spinning seats and serves a mean veal mess. The motorcycle clock over the grill honks and vrooms on the hour. It's right across the street from the Kansas Oil Museum.

Mounted on a rotating pedestal, Valeda is the featured attraction of this center for health, which was started years ago by the Hertzler Foundation, named for Arthur Hertzler, a Kansas doc who traveled the state in a horse and buggy.

Valeda, of course, didn't travel in the buggy. She wasn't even made until 1965, when a German student model in Cologne allowed a transparent rubber compound to be slopped on her body and left until it dried.

Valeda, who is 5-foot-7 and would weigh 145 pounds if she weren't made out of plastic, has several sisters around the country, but according to the folks at the Learning Center, she's the only one who still talks. One of her siblings in Chicago was almost named

Trivia

In 1929 the Haven High football team beat local rival Sylvia High 256–0.

Cassie, the Lassie with the Glassy Chassis. Lucky for Valeda III, who was named after her Chicago sister, they opted for Valeda instead.

To get a personal audience with the transparent woman, visit the Kansas Learning Center for Health at 505 Main Street in Halstead, open 10 a.m. to 4 p.m. Monday through Friday. Admission is $2. Phone (316) 835-2662, www.learningcenter.org.

Has Nike Heard about This?
Hutchinson

If you can run around Hutchinson's Grain Elevator J in less than three minutes and forty-three seconds, you'll have just beaten the world record for a mile. The grain elevator holds eighteen million bushels of wheat (enough to fill 5,400 railroad cars). One lap around the huge concrete structure makes an even mile, and a time of 3:43 or less beats the record set by Hicham El Guerrouj in 1999. Maybe you should try out for the Olympics.

You can find Hutchinson at the intersection of Highways 96 and 61, and you can't miss the grain elevator. Take your running shoes.

Now That's Some Impressive Yard Art
Hutchinson

The Kansas Cosmosphere and Space Center, an affiliate of the Smithsonian, has some yard art you probably won't find at just any Home Depot. I mean, how many yards have you seen with a 70-foot Redstone rocket by the front door? Or a Titan II rocket by the flower garden? The Cosmosphere also has an SR-71 Blackbird, a spyplane that flew at speeds above Mach 3.2; that maybe doesn't qualify as yard art, but you can sure see it from the street.

Started in a poultry barn in 1962, this world-famous space museum has lots of amazing exhibits, including the world's largest collection of space suits, an astronaut training jet, the actual Apollo 13 command module, and a full-scale space shuttle replica. Second

Yard art bigger than the yard.
COURTESY OF COSMOSPHERE

only to D.C.'s National Air and Space Museum in number of space artifacts, the Comosphere also offers space camp for kids of all ages, leases space artifacts to museums all over the world, and even consults with Hollywood when they're filming space movies.

The Cosmosphere is located at 1100 North Plum in Hutchison (800-397-0330; www.cosmo.org).

Lost Shaker of Salt

Hutchinson

California and Alaska had a gold rush. Colorado had a silver boom. In Kansas we had a salt boom. It happened in 1887, soon after Ben Blanchard accidentally discovered salt. He was hoping for oil.

Once the word got out that Kansas had the world's largest piece of salt (it's 100 miles long by 40 miles wide), salt miners flooded to Hutchinson. At one time, there were more than twenty-six salt companies in Hutch, producing up to 44.1 million tons of salt each year. Blocks of salt were cut whole from the 10- to 12-foot veins. Worry all you want about running out of oil, but Hutchinson's 10- to 12-foot veins of pure salt will keep the country in salt for 250,000 years.

Hutch's salt boom came just in the nick of time to save the little town that was started in 1871 by a Baptist minister who marked out the streets with buffalo skulls and threatened to reclaim the deed of any property owner who dared drink hard liquor or even carry it onto his property. Not a popular statute in the wild Kansas frontier.

The Kansas Underground Salt Museum makes Hutchinson the only town in the United States with a museum that's 650 feet below the ground. The museum, still a working salt mine, tells the history of Hutchinson's salt mines and how they played an important role in everything from the Interstate Commerce Commission (the Elkins Act of 1903 was the result of an ICC hearing in Hutch that pitted the "Trusts," nine companies owned by the owner of Morton Salt, against the independent salt producers) to nuclear testing during the Cold War. Thankfully, the tests conducted by the Atomic Energy Commission didn't use real radioactive waste.

Today, there are more than 14,000 uses for salt. The museum, with 100,000 square feet of gallery space, is the only museum in a working salt mine—a mine that stretches for 67 miles, part of which is used (because of its 68-degree temp and 40 percent relative humidity) to store the original reels of classic Hollywood movies. The Kansas Underground Salt Museum is located at 3504 East Avenue G, (620-662-1425; www.undergroundmuseum.org).

Confucius Say: Don't Throw Rocks in Glass Houses
Kechi

If you search on the Internet for Rollin Karg, the industrial engineer turned glassblower, you might think he lives in Miami or Portland or in one of the other 300 cities that have galleries with his work. But you'd be wrong.

Karg, one of the premier glassblowing artists in the world, lives and works in Kechi, Kansas (population 940), in an outdoor studio behind his home.

A former engineer for Cessna, Karg turned his glassblowing skills (he also dabbled for a while in photography and ceramics) into a full-time business in 1983. He and his wife, Patti, who also blows, saw some Steuben glassmakers in Corning, New York.

Rollin said, "Honey, I'd like to try that."

Patti said, "Yeah, sure."

But the next thing she knew, he was signed up for a glassblowing class at Emporia State University.

"He made one paperweight and he hasn't stopped since," says Patti, who runs the business along with Rollin and several glassblowing apprentices.

Visitors can see glass being blown Monday, Tuesday, Thursday, and Friday from 8:30 a.m. to 3 p.m. Or you can tour the gallery

(Karg's works plus those of fifty other artists are displayed) from 8:30 a.m. to 5 p.m. Monday through Saturday. To get there, take exit 14 off I-35 and head 2 miles east. Karg Art Glass is at 111 North Oliver, at 61st and Oliver (316-744-2442).

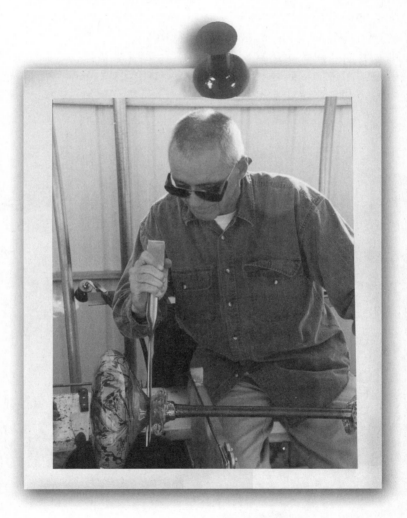

Rollin Karg's "glass act."
ROLLIN KARG

I Do . . . But Only If
Kingman

When Glenn Stark proposed to his wife, she said "sure"—upon one condition: She wanted not a traditional wedding band, but a wedding ring carved from wood. After all, wood carving was such a part of Stark's life that a ring made of anything else would never fly. Besides, to marry Stark would mean living in a basement home with a wooden Will Rogers, Abe Lincoln, a cigar store Indian, and Hagar the Horrible.

The first sign of a grasshopper plague?
STEVE SCHULTZ

Stark, a prolific wood-carver and cement artist, started carving wood as early as second grade. He told his mom that shaping things with his hands was as much a part of him as wanting to breathe. Today, he says he sees ideas in everything.

"I can see designs in veneer on doors. In clouds, in water and animals. I have too many ideas. Almost as many as there are stars," he says.

Although Stark is retired now, he worked in many fields before moving to his unusual home on the outskirts of Kingman. He worked as a Baptist minister, a Navy seaman (he was in Pearl Harbor on December 7, 1941), a carpenter, a stone mason, a bricklayer, and a sign painter.

Even though his artwork can be found in nearly all fifty states, Stark doesn't really consider himself an artist. But I encourage you to take one look at his house in Kingman and then decide. Hagar the Horrible holds the mailbox.

There's also a giant grasshopper, a winged griffin, a Native American couple, a bear on his hind feet, a buffalo, a steer, two prairie dogs, a 4-foot catfish hanging from a tree limb, and two totem poles. And that's just the front yard.

To view more of Stark's art, drive by his house at 1100 Coronado (the corner of Grant and Coronado) in Kingman or head to the Grassroots Art Center in Lucas (213 South Main Street; 785-525-6118).

But Honey, There's a Kangaroo in My Bed . . .
Nickerson

When Sondra Hedrick says to her husband, "This place is a zoo," she isn't kidding. Her husband, Joe, a former rodeo clown and bull-fighter, decided that rather than stock his ranch with the typical cows and chickens, he'd go for kangaroos, zebras, giraffes, yaks, chimpanzees, and pygmy goats.

For years, Hedrick didn't open his unusual ranch to the public, even though it caused more than a few cases of whiplash for travelers

Just two of the permanent residents of Hedrick's Exotic Animal Farm.
HEDRICK'S EXOTIC ANIMAL FARM

zooming down Highway 96. Rather, Hedrick rented out his animals for petting zoos and Christmas parades (his fallow deer make excellent reindeer). He gave camel and pony rides and promoted races of his ostriches, camels, and pigs.

Finally, in 1992, Hedrick gave in. He agreed to open his Exotic Animal Farm on weekends, even added concession facilities and a bed-and-breakfast with a frontier facade of a bank, saloon, grocery store, and livery stable.

And unlike Embassy Suites, where you look out from your room into a courtyard of plants and fountains, at Hedrick's you look out into a courtyard filled with kangaroos and wallabies. It's undoubtedly the most unique bed-and-breakfast anywhere in the world. Each of the eight rooms is decorated in safari motif, with mosquito netting, zebra sheets, painted ostrich eggs, and llama-wool foot warmers. And after a big hearty breakfast, you'll get a tour of Hedrick's 700 animals, or at least those that aren't on the road in a pygmy goat race or a Girl Scout petting zoo somewhere.

If you want to be kissed by a camel or licked by a llama, hurry to Hedrick's Exotic Animal Farm, 8 miles northwest of Hutchinson on Highway 96. The mailing address is 7910 North Roy L. Smith Road, Nickerson, KS 67561. Phone (620) 422-3245 or visit www.hedricks.com.

Beyond the Ce-dar
Partridge

They're not as bad as dandelions, but almost. The eastern red cedar clump along Kansas stream beds, and for farmers who need the pasture, they can sometimes get out of hand. That's where Jay Yoder comes in. Not only will he gladly cut down errant cedars, but he'll drag them home to his workshop barn and turn them into chairs. That people buy.

He calls his creations "twig furniture," and customers snatch them up quicker than they can say "brace and bit," the old-time tools that inspired Jay to start making furniture. Most everything is constructed the old-fashioned way. He even uses square nails that he buys from a company in Maine that has been around since 1810.

"Some people call them 'Goldilocks chairs,'" he says. "Others call them 'limb furniture' or 'rustic furniture.'"

Each of Yoder's creations is unique. Whether it's a loveseat, a courting chair, or a table, Yoder maintains as much of the original tree as possible. And other than the green, he uses every scrap.

A chair made from a genuine tree—who knew?
JAY YODER

"I was at a crafts show and overheard this excited little kid pulling on his mom's sleeve. 'Mom,' he said. 'Come look at this. Chairs made from trees,'" Yoder said.

Yoder's company, the Wooden Anvil Mercantile, can be reached at (620) 567-3102.

"Feeling Fine on Elderberry Wine"
Peck

Forget flu shots! Drink elderberry wine instead. According to an article in *Good Housekeeping,* elderberry wine is every bit as effective at boosting your immune system. Plus, it's a heckuva lot easier (not to mention much more fun) to administer. Hic.

The largest producer of this medicinal wine is located in none other than Peck, Kansas, an hour or so from Carry Nation's hometown of Medicine Lodge. Wyldewood Cellars Winery was started in 1994 by John Brewer, a Ph.D. scientist, and his sister, Merry Brewer, an industrial buyer, neither of whom has had a cold or a virus since they started drinking their own wines. Their mother, a nurse, planted the 1,000-acre family ranch with elderberries in the late 1980s. At the time, she had no idea why, just that she knew they were good for treating everything from upper respiratory infections and diarrhea to sunburns.

John, who made wine as a hobby, decided to try using his mom's elderberries instead of grapes. Eight years and 200 formulas later, he took the results to his friend Mike Martini, a famous Napa Valley winemaker, who couldn't tell the difference between elderberries and grapes.

Hippocrates, who used to prescribe elderberries back in the fifth century BC, would be pleased. In fact the Romans used to say that anyone who grew elderberries would die of old age rather than illness.

If that's the case, the Brewers, who in only fifteen years have already landed 500 awards for their wines (including a sales-boosting "best buy" in *Wine Enthusiast* magazine and being served at the 2002 Winter Olympics), will need to buy a bigger ranch just to house all their awards.

Wyldewood Cellars Winery also makes elderberry jams and jellies, elderberry concentrate, and wines from blackberries and native Kansas sand plums. It's open 9 a.m. to 6 p.m., Monday through Saturday and noon to 5 p.m. on Sunday. Take exit 33 off the Kansas Turnpike. Call (800) 711-9748 or visit www.wyldewoodcellars.com for more information.

Spanky and Our Gang Are Alive and Well in Kansas
Pretty Prairie

You won't find any computer-generated special effects in the Pretty Prairie Civic Theatre. No subtitles. No body-ripping explosions. Just good old-fashioned movies with the emphasis being on *old*. Old as in 16-millimeter film. Old as in *Harvey, Ma and Pa Kettle at the Fair, High Noon,* and *Casablanca.*

There's no neon marquee. The seats are wooden, and every movie is preceded by a classic cartoon such as *Felix the Cat,* and an "Our Gang" short with Carl "Alfalfa" Switzer, the freckle-faced kid with the lick of hair that stands up straight.

Alfalfa, it seems, used to be a local. After he got too old for "Our Gang," he married a local gal whose dad owned the town's feed store, then bought a farm a few miles north of here.

Like many towns, Pretty Prairie had a movie theater in the Hollywood-crazy 1920s and '30s. The Civic, so named because the city owned it and split the proceeds with movie exhibitors, was pushed aside in the '50s for television.

The Civic, unlike theaters in many towns, didn't get sold and cut up into other businesses after its last screening in March 1955. In fact when Darrell Albright moved home to Pretty Prairie in 1980 to open a grocery store, he was dumbstruck by what he found inside the brick building a couple doors down.

Thanks to Darrell Albright, the curtain will never come down on the Pretty Prairie Civic Theatre.

DARRELL ALBRIGHT

The 16-millimeter projectors, the steel-lined projection booth, the 212 wooden seats, the puny 8-by-10-foot screen, and the ancient fire curtain with hand-painted advertisements for local businesses were all still there, just like they were twenty-five years before. It seems the city, other than allowing a few meetings up front and an annual Santa Claus show, had pretty much left it alone. Darrell even found the original theater speaker underneath piles of city papers. He plugged it in and, remarkably, it still worked.

★ ★

Aware of the Alfalfa connection, and the fact that the movie *Wait Till the Sun Shines, Nellie* was shot in Pretty Prairie in 1951, Albright decided it was time to reopen the theater.

As for Alfalfa, he didn't fare so well. He divorced the local gal, moved back to California, became a hunting guide and a bartender, and fell on hard times. In 1958 he was arrested for cutting down Christmas trees in Sequoia National Park. A month later, Alfie, as friends still called him, was shot in the stomach over a $50 debt.

Almost sounds like a movie, one that would be guaranteed a long run in Pretty Prairie.

The Pretty Prairie Civic Theatre is located on the south side of Main Street. Movies are shown most Saturdays at 7:30 p.m. Admission $5 for adults, $3 for children under twelve. For more info, call Darrell Albright at (620) 459-4600.

Pyramid Power
Wichita

If you have a spare two grand and want to rent a pyramid for your next business meeting, consider the Bob Page Pyramid at Wichita's Center for the Improvement of Human Functioning. The pyramid, originally built for experiments with energy, is now regular old meeting space that accommodates 200 tables.

You might suspect that a pyramid in the middle of Wichita could seem a bit jarring, but at the Center for the Improvement of Human Functioning, it fits right in. The rest of the center's eight buildings are geodesic domes, designed by the late great humanist Buckminster Fuller to be energy efficient and require no internal support. There's not a right angle anywhere on the center's four acres. Even the road leading up to Dome 1, where you'll find the Taste of Health restaurant, the Gift of Health gift store, and a sign that declares, SOME OF THE MOST WONDERFUL PEOPLE PASS THROUGH THESE DOORS, is highly curved and is flanked by signs that say DESTRESS TO 25 MPH.

The mission of the center (aka the Bright Spot for Health) is to stimulate an epidemic of health. Their forty-five full-time doctors, therapists, and researchers treat up to 500 patients a year in holistic and natural medicine. The center was started in 1975 by Olive W. Garvey, an innovative thinker who at sixty-five became CEO of her husband's business, Garvey Inc.

Tours of the unique facility at 3100 North Hillside Avenue are given Monday through Friday at 1:30 p.m. A nutritious, fiber-laden lunch can be had between 11:30 a.m. and 1:30 p.m. at Taste of Health. Phone (316) 682-3100 or visit www.brightspot.org.

The Great Pyramid of Wichita.
GREATER WICHITA CONVENTION AND VISITORS BUREAU

★ ★

Trivia

Arnold Schwarzenegger, former he-man and governor of California, sent his 1987 Wagoneer to Wichita so Jonathan Goodwin, self-described gearhead, could convert it from running on normal gasoline to biodiesel, doubling its fuel efficiency. Goodwin converts about six cars a month. A recent project was turning Neil Young's 1959 Lincoln Continental into a plug-in hybrid that gets up to 100 mpg.

That Slant in Your "F" Indicates an Aloof and Impartial Demeanor

Wichita

If you're a handwriting analyst, you could do worse than plunking down the $8.95 admission fee for the Museum of World Treasures. There, you can analyze the signatures of the first forty-three U.S. presidents (they're still waiting for Obama's), Joe DiMaggio, Peter the Great, Charles Dickens, Sir Isaac Newton, rocker Charlie Daniels, and many famous historical figures.

This three-story brick museum with all the famous signatures started as the personal collection of Dr. Jon Kardatzke, a Wichita physician who finally consented to share his forty-year collection with the public after friends kept insisting. His unique presidential signatures collection started with an autograph of Thomas Jefferson that he picked up at an auction in Beverly Hills while completing his Roman Caesar gold and silver coin collection. After he had all the presidents, he expanded into European royalty, authors, composers, scientists, and military leaders.

At the museum that Kardatzke first opened in a former Holiday Inn (he has since moved to a building five times as large),

You look like death warmed over . . .
GREATER WICHITA CONVENTION AND VISITORS BUREAU

handwriting analysts can supplement their research with other Kardatzke antiquities, some more than hundreds of millions of years old. Among other things, Kardatzke's collection includes one of only four complete *Tyrannosaur albertosaurus* skeletons in the world, a Mayan burial urn, the shrunken head of a nineteenth-century Ecuadorian man that was once worn around the neck for good luck, an Egyptian mummy from the royal tombs in Thebes, and the silver bowl from which Hitler ate his last meal before committing suicide.

Kardatzke got interested in collecting coins when he was sixteen. You know those T-shirts, MY PARENTS WENT TO JERUSALEM AND ALL I GOT WAS THIS CRUMMY T-SHIRT. Well, Kardatzke's parents were smart enough to bring back something more compelling when they visited the Holy Lands in 1956—six gold Roman coins, including one of Herod the Great that, Kardatzke says, "infected me with a love for ancient history for life."

A few years later, Kardatzke's parents took the kids along on a trip to Greece, and Jon, who was scraping around near the Acropolis, found a cup handle buried in the soil. A Greek official grabbed him by the shoulder and informed him that digging was prohibited, but let him keep the cup handle anyway. He has been hooked ever since.

The 36,000-square-foot Museum of World Treasures is located in the Farm and Art Market in Old Town at 835 East First Street (316-263-1311; www.worldtreasures.org).

Harold and Kumar Should Have Gone to NuWay
Wichita

It's no big secret that Wichita is the "Air Capital of the World." Since 1919, more than 250 million planes have been built here, including the first commercial plane (the Laird Swallow), the first business jet (Bill Lear forsook Switzerland for Wichita when launching his LearJet), and more than 40 percent of the airplanes in the sky today.

Another stellar distinction that Wichita claims is not quite as well known. Wichita also happens to be the "Fast Food Chain Capital of the World." Or, rather, more fast food chains were launched here than in any other city in America. Pizza Hut, of course, was started in Wichita in 1958. But long before that (1921, to be exact), the very first fast food hamburger chain was launched in Wichita. Yes, White Castle began in Wichita when Walter Anderson, a cook, and Billy Ingram, a real estate agent, formed the White Castle System of Eating Houses. This, I hasten to point out, was thirty-three years before Ray Kroc even met the McDonald brothers.

Although White Castle didn't gain quite the financial status as its yellow-arched imitator, it was the first to establish uniformity (can you say chain?) at its many locations. Although White Castle eventually bailed and set up headquarters in Ohio, no one argues that it was the first fast food chain restaurant.

Since then, Wichita has spawned a plethora of fast food chains, including Spangles, Bionic Burger, and my personal favorite, NuWay Cafe. I prefer NuWay because it contents itself to remain small and local. At last count, there were only five NuWays, all in Wichita, all serving the restaurant's trademark crumbly ground beef sandwiches and homemade root beer. You often have to wait for a seat at the vintage U-shaped counter with the vinyl and metal stools.

If you want to see the restaurant that a writer for *National Geographic* raved about, visit the original NuWay at 1416 West Douglas Avenue (316-267-1131; www.nuwaycafe.com).

Trivia

Before he became a legend of the Old West, Wyatt Earp served as a police constable in Wichita. His main responsibility was rounding up stray dogs. Earp had a bad habit of pocketing the fines he collected rather than turning them in to the city, so when he left for Dodge City in 1872, the accounting office withheld his last paycheck.

Kansas Wins the Pennant for . . . New York?

On July 28, 1911, Charles Victory Faust, a thirty-year-old hayseed from Wichita, showed up on a practice field for the New York Giants. They were in St. Louis preparing to play the Cardinals. Faust, wearing a black suit and a tall black hat, approached John McGraw, the manager for the Giants, and informed him that a psychic had told him that if he pitched for the Giants, they'd win the pennant. McGraw, who believed in omens and charms, decided to give the man a chance. After a couple of pitches, it was obvious that Faust not only knew nothing about pitching (he used an odd double windmill), but that he'd never played the game of baseball. Nevertheless, as the team was boarding the train for a stand against Chicago the next day, Faust was there, complete with uniform. He dressed, ate, practiced, and traveled with the team from that day on. Although he was only allowed to play one inning against the last-place Dodgers, McGraw gave Faust credit for, sure enough, winning the pennant that year.

Faust stayed on the team, and the Giants won the pennant for the next three years. In 1915, Faust died in a hospital for the insane, and the Giants, who suffered their first losing season in fifteen years, finished in last place.

Einstein's Brain Slept Here

When Albert Einstein died in 1955, his body was cremated. Twenty years later, while reading through some of Einstein's papers, an editor from the *New Jersey Monthly* noticed that Einstein had requested that his brain be preserved. No one at the small Princeton hospital where he'd died knew anything about it. In 1978, the editor sent a reporter to find out what had happened to the famous scientist's brain. The reporter eventually tracked down a Princeton pathologist, Dr. Thomas S. Harvey, who had indeed removed the brain. When the reporter found Dr. Harvey, he was working in Wichita at a medical testing lab. After much pressing, Dr. Harvey reached into a cupboard, pulled out a cardboard box labeled *Costa Cider,* and withdrew two Mason jars filled with formaldehyde and bits and pieces of Einstein's brain. Scientific studies were performed on the brain, although Dr. Harvey, who now lives in Florida, still has most of it. In 1997, he put the brain in a Tupperware container, stuck it in the trunk of a rented car, and drove to Berkeley, California, to show the brain to Einstein's granddaughter.

Pizza Mixed in Baby's Bathtub Becomes World's Largest Restaurant Chain

Wichita

One night in the late 1950s, while Frank and Dan Carney were working in their widowed mom's Wichita grocery store, a fight broke out at the bar next door. The landlord of that building, fed up with noisy tenants, suggested to the elder Carney that her sons, students at Wichita State University, open a small, quiet restaurant there instead.

★ ★

Borrowing $600 from their mother, the Carney boys, ages nine-teen and twenty-four, decided to serve a popular new food called pizza. While mom sewed red-and-white-checkered curtains, the young men rounded up a baby's bathtub in which to mix the dough. They also hustled an old oven that eventually melted the handles off the door. They named their restaurant Pizza Hut, mainly because that's all they could fit on the sign used by the building's former occupant, the B&B Lounge.

From the day it opened in the summer of 1958, the pizzeria was a success. Within a few months, the college boys were raking in $1,000 a week, and by 1977 they had sold it to PepsiCo for a cool $300 million.

The first Pizza Hut was located at Kellogg and Bluff Streets, but it has been moved to the campus of Wichita State University near the entrance at 17th and Hillside Streets.

Dem Bones
Winfield

By day, he's a diesel mechanic. By night and just about any other time he can find a spare moment, Barry Patton is one of the world's premier double-fisted bones players. Yes, I said bones—as in skel-etons, as in dense, hard, calcified tissue. And yes, Patton has played this unusual musical instrument with everyone from country singer Vince Gill to the Louisville Philharmonic Orchestra. He even sells a bones video teaching wannabes how to master the rare percus-sion instrument that originated in Egypt in 1600 BC. Bone rattlers, as they're called, traditionally used cattle ribs, but in medieval Europe, oxen ribs were all the rage. Barry has preferred to make most of his fifteen sets of bones out of hedgewood, although he still plays the set given to him by the old-timer who taught him how to play nearly forty years ago.

When Barry was fourteen, bones player Cecil Hiatt (known far and wide as Oklahoma Bones after he picked up the skill from an

Old West medicine show) accidentally slammed Barry's finger in a car door. He felt so bad that he gave Barry a set of bones to make up for it. Barry, thanks to the broken finger that required a splint, had lots of time to practice.

Cecil saw promise in his young student, so he took Barry under his wing. As Barry says now, "Bones have taken me to more places and introduced me to more friends than I ever dreamed possible."

Catch Barry's act at the Walnut Valley Festival in Winfield the third weekend in September, or order a video or your own set of bones by calling (620) 221-0660 or logging on to www.doublestop.com/barrybones.htm.

Kansas Was His First Inspiration

Frederic Remington, the famous western artist of some 3,000 sketches, paintings, and sculptures, got so bored on his 160-acre sheep farm outside Whitewater that he began sketching cowboy scenes, some on the door of a neighbor's barn.

Originally from back East, Remington moved to Kansas in 1883 on a "get rich quick" mission. A friend from Yale insisted there was money to be made in sheep farming, an occupation that didn't appeal to Remington for much longer than nine months. After running a bar and a grocery store in Kansas City, he finally convinced his childhood sweetheart to marry him. By 1885, they were back in New York, and Remington was selling his cowboy sketches to *Harpers Weekly* and other magazines.

Modern-day Land Rush
Winfield

Land rushes, a popular method for distributing property in the late 1800s, are still popular in Winfield, at least every September, when thousands of campers line up to find the best camping spot for the annual Walnut Valley Festival. They come up to three weeks early to get their numbers and await the 8 a.m. starting gun that marks Land

The Walnut Valley Festival—where Florida's
pink flamingos go to retire!

Rush, which starts an entire week before the official music begins.

The festival, a nearly four-decade tradition that attracts the country's best acoustic musicians, features six stages of nonstop music, a big arts and crafts exhibit, and four days of national flat-picking championships. But the festivalgoers, many of whom haven't missed a single one, are the real troupers. They decorate their campsites with intense planning that would give Martha Stewart pause. There are castles, tropical paradises, "log cabins," and re-creations of granny's back porch.

Walnut Valley Festival is held the third weekend of September at the Cowley County fairgrounds. Call (620) 221-3250 for more info, or check out the festival's Web site at www.wvfest.com.

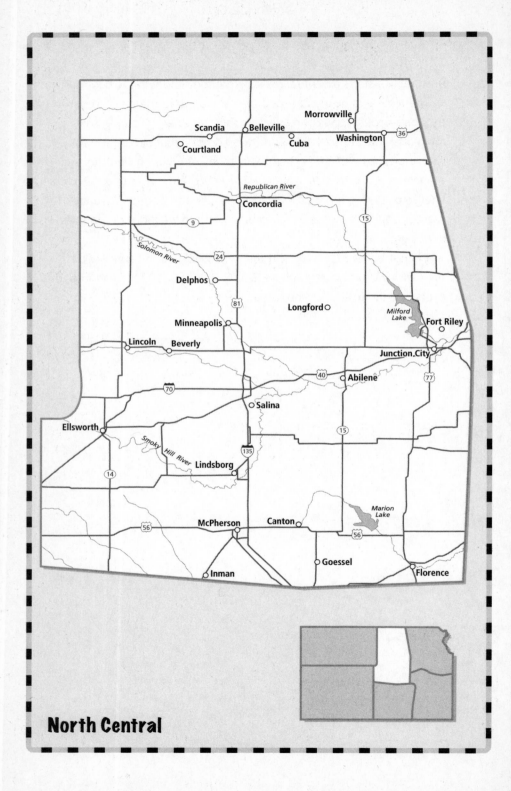

North Central

5

North Central

Dwight D. Eisenhower, *five-star general and thirty-fourth president of the United States, used to say that the proudest thing he could claim was being from Abilene.*

After reading about his stomping ground in north central Kansas, I think you'll see why. North central Kansas boasts such natural wonders as house-size rocks, buffalo herds that run wild, real cowboys, and a proud military history that goes back to the U.S. Cavalry.

And if that wasn't enough, Ike's hometown of Abilene holds the stellar distinction of owning the world's largest spur, a spur so big that two Chevy Silverados, each with a load of sixteen screaming cheerleaders, can drive underneath it at the same time. But what's even more amazing is that the ginormous spur, fashioned from an antiquated swamp cooler, wasn't even there to add to Ike's pride. The award-winning spur didn't get erected until three decades after the famous Kansan's death.

And while I'd hate to start any rumors, there's also a scintillating underwear show in Junction City, just 30 miles northeast of Abilene.

★ ★

Homeopathy for Beginners
Abilene

If you had a bunion, a backache, or a sick horse back in 1899, there's a good chance you'd turn to A. B. Seelye. After all, he's the guy who came up with Wasa-Tusa, Fro-zona, Ner-Vena, and hundreds of other home remedies that back in those days answered that perennial question: How do you spell relief?

From Abilene, Kansas, where he ran the A. B. Seelye Medical Company, the crafty entrepreneur dispersed 400 wagons carrying one hundred patent medicines to a fourteen-state area. Back then, it was the biggest medicine company in the country, the equivalent of Eli Lilly today.

"The label on Wasa-Tusa said it cured anything," said Terry Tietjens, who bought the Seelye mansion and lived there with Seelye's two unmarried daughters after they got too old to run the place. "You used it for your cold, your horse, your wife—it didn't matter."

The old vats and recipes for all of Seelye's cure-alls (from salves, potions, and lotions to talcum powder, perfume, and extracts) are on display at the Patent Medicine Museum. Most folks come to ooh and aah at the mansion, a twenty-five-room beauty with a bowling alley in the basement and what some say is the world's largest nutcracker

* *

collection (they're put out every Christmas), but I'm partial to the crazy medicines, most of which contained 87 percent alcohol.

To see the medicines that were "good for man or beast," visit the Patent Medicine Museum, located behind the mansion at 1105 North Buckeye Street in Abilene. Phone (785) 263-1084 or visit www.seelyemansion.org.

The cure for what ails you!
TERRY TIETJENS, SEELYE MANSION

★ ★

Fits and Spurs
Abilene

Heaven knows, a writer of *Curiosities* books is keenly aware of all the giant creatures along America's byways, from Bimijidi, Wisconsin's 10-foot Babe, the Blue Ox, to Blanchester, Ohio's 68-foot Hermit Crab (the Freedom Worship Baptist Church that owns it claims sixty people can sit within its shell), but I've yet to see one big enough to

Get along, big dogies.
JACQUE KARL, CENTRAL KANSAS FREE FAIR ASSOCIATION

need the 28-foot spur, the world's largest, owned by Abilene's Wild Bill Hickok Rodeo Arena. They didn't have any trouble landing the stellar designation from the Guinness folks, being as there's not a lot of competition. Abilene, Texas, of course, has the world's largest Spur and Bit Show, and Waco, Texas, recently sold in an auction what they called the world's largest collection of spurs (including a double diamond pair worn by John Wayne), but nobody seems to be in the running for the title of world's largest singular spur. Weighing in at more than 2,000 pounds, the Abilene spur is an impressive piece of hardware, big enough for a semi-truck and a trailer to pass under with nary a scratch.

Originally constructed in New Mexico out of a derelict swamp cooler, the monstrous spur came to Kansas with Larry Houston, who built it after watching a friend's little boy drive a toy truck under a normal-size spur. He sold it to the Central Kansas Free Fair folks, who immediately recognized its potential. Drive under the spur at the north end of the fairgrounds arena, Pine and Northwest Eighth.

We Are Family
Belleville

Next time you're trying to decide which new toy will best spark your six-year-old's creativity, think of the Boyer family in Belleville.

Edward and Delia, who raised ten kids on a farm south of Belleville, refused to give their kids toys. Instead they gave them free access to the shop, the junk pile, and the tools.

Over and over, Edward told his kids, "You've got to create your own entertainment. If you want something, you can make it."

No sooner did his eight boys learn to walk, then they learned to carve, build, and make motors. Their two sisters learned to paint and make crafts.

When Paul Boyer was ten, Edward took the family to the fair. While the rest of the kids spent their money on rides, Paul spent his allotment returning again and again to the same sideshow—a carver

★ ★

who made puppets out of wood. When he was twelve, he created his first motion machine—a kitchen scene where the mom churned butter, the kids played music, and the chickens picked up scratch. It moved by a shaft heated from the kitchen stove.

Since then, he's made hundreds of motion machines. For a while, he worked in Detroit at a lumberyard; carving and making motors was just a hobby. But in 1965, he lost his leg and contracted hepatitis from a blood transfusion. Doctors gave him five years to live.

Instead of dwelling on the grim prognosis, Paul remembered his dad's advice to make his own entertainment. Working from a

Frenetic fancy.
JAMES S. DICK

wheelchair, he devoted himself full-time to the animated carvings and elaborate motion machines.

He's still at it today.

"I've got so many ideas, I'm at least ten years behind schedule," he says.

Paul still collects parts for his inventions the same way he did as a child—by rummaging through junk piles. Appliance dealers save timers from old dryers. Local folks bring boxes of old clockworks. He has even been known to filch necklaces from his wife's jewelry box.

Six decades of Paul's work are showcased in the Paul Boyer Museum of Animated Carvings. Twenty-five lighted display cases, each wired with a timer button to send the whimsical creations into action, show such elaborate scenes as hillbillies making moonshine, a woman on her exercise bike, Indians doing a war dance, and a blacksmith trying to shoe a kicking horse. Housed in a renovated ice cream factory, this fascinating museum is run by Paul's daughters, Ann Lewellyn and Candy Sanford. The museum is located at 1205 M Street in Belleville. Call (785) 527-5884 for information.

Trick or Treat

Beverly

After writing several books about roadside oddities, I have come to the conclusion that making animals out of farm implements is not that out-of-the-ordinary. In fact, I'd venture to bet there's not a state among us that doesn't have at least one or two zoos full of rusted-out lathes and motorcycle gas tanks. Not that every last one of them isn't impressive.

But when I found out about Jim Dickerman's Open Range Zoo, off Kansas Highway 18, I knew I was on to something unique. For one thing, Dickerman's zoo has the world's largest dragon. Jim's Dream Dragon IV, made from an antique McCormick threshing machine, is 60 feet long and 20 feet tall. Its tail even moves up and down in the wind. Not only that, but all of Dickerman's scrap metal animals glow

★ ★

in the dark. Most creators of discarded-metal menageries are content to leave them rusted and weathered.

Dream Dragon IV is at mile marker 106 off Highway 18, about 0.5 mile east of Beverly. But if you want to see all of Jim's outdoor creations (the Kansas Canary, Bug Lady, and Break Out, to name a few), pick up a map at the Grassroots Art Center in Lucas (785-525-6118).

I'll give you two guesses. Which one is Jim Dickerman?
STEVE SCHULTZ

Before Daytona

On his nineteenth birthday, four-time NASCAR champ Jeff Gordon took his first national Midget Title in Belleville on the town's famous Belleville High Banks. Built in 1910, this 0.5-mile dirt track, billed as the world's fastest, has hosted horses and motorcycles, as well as such famous race car champs as Parnelli Jones, A. J. Foyt, Tony Stewart, and, of course, Gordon, who "ran wide open, jumped the cushion, and never stopped lifting" for his Midget Title in 1990.

Happy Birthday, Mr. Gordon.
JAMES S. DICK

★ ★

Trivia

When new townsites in Kansas were surveyed and plotted, promoters commonly offered a free lot to the first house in the new "city." A. F. Horner built a house in Brookville and then sledged it across the plains to Florence, and on to Newton and then Hutchinson.

Where the Buffalo Roam
Canton

If you go to the Bronx Zoo, you'll probably hear a story or two about William Hornaday. He was the zoo's first director, an avid conservationist, and the guy who started the American Bison Society at the zoo's Lion House in 1905.

He started the A.B.S. because buffalo that once roamed American prairies were threatened with extinction. Thanks to frontiersmen like Wyatt Earp and Bat Masterson, who shot them for $3 a hide, the 1905 buffalo census reported a mere 1,000 buffalo left. Hard to believe there were once 70 million of them. Some herds in the good old days were as big as the state of Rhode Island.

Hornaday was savvy enough to recognize that if somebody didn't step in, the once prolific buffalo would soon be gone forever. In fact, the herd he started at the zoo in October 1899 eventually restocked bison herds in Oklahoma, Montana, South Dakota, and Nebraska.

I tell you this story to illustrate a point. Kansas also had a conservationist who recognized the need to preserve buffalo. In fact, the Kansan rounded up his herd of bison in 1859, when Hornaday was only four years old. But how many people have heard of John Gault Maxwell?

★ ★

If you go to the Maxwell Wildlife Refuge, a 2,800-acre preserve north of Canton, you'll probably hear about Maxwell and see 200 descendants of his herd, which was willed by the family to Kansas Wildlife and Parks.

The refuge also has elk, a 20-foot lookout tower, a 1½-mile hiking trail, and a forty-six-acre fishing lake. Show up on a weekend (be sure to call ahead) and you can even ride on what Friends of Maxwell call a "modern-day covered wagon." It's actually a tram that seats twenty, but boy, are you in for a treat: bison, wildflowers, and prairie just as it was 200 years ago.

If you give them enough notice, the Friends of Maxwell will even serve you a campfire barbecued buffalo dinner, complete with beans, potato salad, and cobbler.

The Maxwell Wildlife Refuge is 6 miles north of Canton on 27th Avenue. Call (620) 628-4455 or check out www.cyberkraft.com/maxwell.

Napoleon's Own Curtain

Concordia

You can go to the Hall of Battles in the Palace of Versailles to see Horace Vernet's famous painting of Napoleon at Austerlitz. Or you can head to Concordia, Kansas, where the painting is displayed on a three-story, 32-foot-wide curtain.

Napoleon "made it" to Kansas thanks to a turn of events that started in the late 1800s. It seems one Colonel Napoleon Bonaparte Brown (no relation to the French general) moved to Concordia to open a bank. By 1900, the town had prospered thanks to its four major railroads, and the rich banker decided it needed a grand opera house. On September 17, 1907, the magnificent 650-seat theater with eight box seats and two balconies opened for a performance of *The Vanderbilt Cup.*

Much to Brown's surprise, his son Earl presented him with the gigantic curtain bearing a picture of his namesake. Unfortunately,

★ ★

both men died within a few years and their widows, who didn't get along, sold the stunning theater. It survived by showing movies until seven decades later, when someone got the harebrained idea to restore it.

By this time, the giant curtain had suffered rain damage ("Napoleon looked like he was having a bad mascara day," says former curator Susie Haver), so $9,000 was raised to make a reproduction.

The Brown Grand Theatre is open Tuesday through Friday. It's located at the west end of downtown, 310 West Sixth Street. For a schedule of events or theater tours, call (785) 243-2553 or visit www.browngrand.org.

Take That, Andy Warhol
Cuba

For a town of barely 200, Cuba has gotten more than its fifteen minutes of fame. In the past decade, this little Czech community where you can see one end of Main Street from the other has been featured twice on CBS and once in an eighteen-page spread in *National Geographic*. Maybe it's because its annual March fund-raiser (a rock-a-thon with seven days of nonstop hours of dueling rocking chairs) is, well, a curiosity. Eighty miles from the nearest mall, Cuba's denizens have also been known to stage frog races and blindfolded lawn mower sprints and ride horses into bars.

Maybe it's because you can't get authentic Czech bologna and jaternice just anywhere. Or maybe it's because its historic Ceska Narodni Sin (Bohemian National Hall) has a backdrop of Prague's Old Town Square, a roller rink, and a senior citizens' center, and, at one time or another, has hosted high school football games and Lawrence Welk. Check out *National Geographic* photographer Jim Richardson's photos of Cuba in Cuba Antiques & Collectibles, 319 Baird, or call (785) 729-3632 to volunteer for a half-hour time slot in the world-famous Cuba Rock-a-Thon. Oh, and if you're wondering why

Working the counter at the Cuba Cash Store.
JAMES S. DICK

a community of Czech-speaking immigrants would name their town
Cuba, no one really knows, but the most popular theory is that a
visitor entranced the settlers with tales of Cubans fighting the Spanish for their freedom, a cause they knew well after escaping a region
under Austria's thumb.

165

Show Me Your Pinky's

In Courtland (pop. 304), the grill fires up around noon at Pinky's, a chicken fried steak and half-pound burger institution on the dirt main street, where it's a pretty sure bet that there will be at least one table of locals playing pinochle. Pinky, who still shows up for work every day even though he sold it to JoAnne Kenyon in 1994, refuses to reveal the secret behind his nickname (anybody who ever knew is dead and gone), but this much we do know: Pinky's is the only place in the world that sells french-fried green beans.

In the Pink–y's.
JAMES S. DICK

First Presidential Fashion Advisor

Delphos

Lincoln's famous Cooper Union Address, the speech that propelled his bid for presidency, was first given and practiced in Kansas. Between November 30 and December 7, 1859, Lincoln toured Kansas, giving the same basic Cooper Union speech in Troy, Doniphan, Atchison, and Elwood.

Grace Bedell, an eleven-year-old girl from New York who later moved to Kansas, really liked the Republican candidate, but she thought his image needed some polishing. She wrote him a letter a month before the election, suggesting strongly that, with his skinny frame, he ought to try a beard.

"All the ladies like whiskers," she wrote, "and they would tease their husbands to vote for you." She also mentioned that although several of her brothers were going to vote for him no matter what he looked like, she thought she could persuade a couple of her other brothers to vote for him if he grew a beard.

Ever gracious Abe wrote her a letter thanking her for the fashion advice, and sure enough, by the time he was inaugurated, he was sporting a full beard, the first American president ever to do so.

Bedell treasured her letter from Lincoln and stored it in a vault in the bank her husband ran in Delphos. Despite offers as high as $5,000, she refused to part with it. Finally, after her death, a television producer bought the famous note for $20,000. Today, a copy of both her original letter and the one Lincoln wrote back are part of a memorial at the northwest corner of City Park on the town square.

Yippee Ti Yi Yea

Ellsworth

Calling all C.O.W.B.O.Y.s—that's Cock-eyed Old West Band of Yahoos, a society started in 1996 by Jim Gray.

Gray started the society to celebrate the rich ranching heritage in Kansas.

"People think of Kansas as the wheat state," Gray says. "But our number one industry is cattle, and you don't handle cattle without cowboys. Ranching has been and still is important to Kansas."

So far, 1,500 rowdies have signed on, including cowboy reenactors, Western songwriters, cowboy poets, and hundreds of armchair cowboys.

Like lots of young boys, Gray, whose family owned a ranch in nearby Geneseo, grew up dreaming about Hopalong Cassidy, Roy Rogers, and Gene Autry. When he was three or four, his mom frantically called around the neighborhood, looking for her lost son. A neighbor finally spotted him, three quarters of a mile away, riding his stick pony up the drive.

"I wanted to be where Roy Rogers was," Gray says.

It wasn't until he was in college at Fort Hays State that he finally put two and two together and figured out that Ellsworth, his own stomping grounds, had about as many cowboys as you could get.

In the late 1800s, drovers herding longhorns on the Chisholm Trail landed in Ellsworth by the thousands. Every other business was a saloon, and Prairie Rose, a famous dance hall girl, staged reenactments of Lady Godiva right down the main drag. Even Wild Bill Hickok couldn't get elected. He lost a close race for sheriff and then town constable to Chauncey Whitney, who is buried in the Ellsworth Cemetery.

To join the C.O.W.B.O.Y. Society, send $18.67 (that's the year the Chisholm Trail came through Kansas with herds of Texas longhorns) to Gray at P.O. Box 62, Ellsworth, KS 67439. You'll get a membership card and a subscription to Kansas Cowboy, a bimonthly newsletter. Phone (785) 472-4703 or visit www.drovers mercantile.com. And remember, "Never sell yer saddle."

Fine Dining, Harvey Style
Florence

If you saw Judy Garland in the movie *Harvey Girls,* you already know about the famous waitresses who wore black dresses and white aprons and could serve a four-course dinner in thirty minutes flat. But you might not know that the first hotel opened by Fred Harvey was located in Florence, Kansas.

Called the Clifton House, the majestic hotel opened in 1878 with fine china, silver, and furniture imported from Europe. The chef, Bill Phillips, even left a job with Chicago's tony Palmer House to come to Florence, where he paid local kids to supply him with prairie chickens and quail.

The Clifton House, which survived only twenty-two years, was reopened in 1971 as a museum. You can even get an original five-course Harvey House meal (using authentic Fred Harvey recipes) served by waitresses (volunteers from the Historical Society) dressed in the old black-and-white outfits.

The Clifton House (now officially known as the Harvey House) is located at 221 Marion Street. To make reservations for a five-course dinner (roast sirloin of beef, mashed potatoes, asparagus with cheese, Fred Harvey coleslaw, relish plate, fruit tray, fresh-baked rolls, and peach charlotte), call (620) 878-4496 or (620) 878-4355.

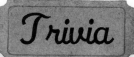

Trivia

Our sixteenth president, who visited Kansas in 1859 while brushing up his Cooper Union speech, remarked that if he ever decided to move west, he'd hightail it straight to Kansas.

★ ★

Hail to the Chief

Fort Riley

When Chief, the last cavalry horse on government rolls, died in 1968, the Army gave him a proper burial with full military honors. The color guard showed up, the commanding general gave a speech, and a Cavalry band at his graveside played such military hits as "Hit the Leather," "Block Horse Troop," and "Sabre and Spurs."

They even buried him standing straight up, with full military tack, including blanket rolls, canteen, and rifle. The vault is underground, so you can't exactly see Chief, but a statue, *Old Trooper Bill,* modeled after Frederic Remington's pencil sketch *The Cavalryman,* marks the grave.

The proud bay gelding's burial site is catty-corner to the Custer House, the native limestone military home (or one just like it) that General George Custer and his wife, Libby, lived in while stationed here in 1866. Right across the parade field is the U.S. Cavalry Museum, which recounts a proud history of America's military horse soldiers that served from the Revolutionary War until 1950.

To see the ghost rider, take exit 301 off I-70 and follow it to the Main Post. You'll see the clock tower for the U.S. Cavalry Museum and 270 historic stone buildings. Phone (785) 239-2737; www.riley.army.mil.

As If One Cracked Bell Wasn't Enough

Goessel

On April 1, 1996, Taco Bell ran an ad in several American newspapers. The ad reported that the Taco Bell Corporation, in an effort to reduce the national debt, had purchased the Liberty Bell and was renaming it the Taco Liberty Bell.

The public, not noticing the April Fool's Day date, was outraged, just as they should be. Even though it's cracked, the Liberty Bell is a proud symbol of American freedom. It's such a great symbol the Smithsonian Institution commissioned the Mennonite Heritage Museum in Goessel to make a full-scale replica of the Liberty Bell out of Turkey Red wheat.

For whom the wheat bell tolls.
SCHMIDT STUDIO AND MENNONITE HERITAGE MUSEUM

Designed by Marie and Martha Voth, twin sisters who also happen to be straw artists, the wheat bell is the spitting image of the one that, despite Taco Bell's claims, still hangs in Philadelphia.

Members of the Mennonite community near Goessel spent 2,000 hours weaving the straw bell. Although it sat in the Smithsonian for several years, it's now back in Kansas at the museum's Turkey Red Wheat Palace. The Wheat Palace also tells the history of the 400 Ukrainians who immigrated to the area in 1874 from Alexanderwohl in Russia, each carrying a bushel of wheat.

The Mennonite Heritage Museum is located at Highway 15, 11 miles north of Newton on I-35. Call (620) 367-8200 or visit www.skyways.org/museums/goessel for more info.

★ ★

Grassroots Tourism
Inman

The only reason people think Kansas is flat and dull is because nobody has bothered to tell them otherwise.

But here's the deal. The only real difference between Kansas and, say, Arizona is an $8 million advertising budget. We have natural wonders, award-winning golf courses, we even have our own Grand Canyon. It's called Arikarae Breaks, and the only reason you've never heard of it is because our boys in Topeka can't see the value in getting the word out.

If Arikarae Breaks, Rock City, or Monument Rocks were in any other state, there would be fancy brochures, tour guides, and million-dollar Web sites. Half of our natural wonders are on dirt roads, in the middle of some cattle rancher's pasture. To get close enough to take a photo, you often have to crawl over barbed wire or retaining walls. I guess the flip side is you don't have smelly, diesel-belching tour buses blocking your view.

About twenty years ago, Mil and Marci Penner decided to correct this glaring deficiency. They figured if legislators couldn't see fit to pony up line items for an advertising budget, they'd just do it themselves. They'd settle for word of mouth, start a grassroots effort.

They'd publish tour guides—whole books, mind you—with listings of things to do in Kansas. The first step was convincing Kansans themselves they had something to offer.

"The going notion was that if you wanted culture or something to do, you'd have to go to Denver or Kansas City," says Marci, who has become a missionary to the uninformed of Kansas.

When their Kansas Weekend Guide, the first of several books, came out in 1990, they staged what they thought would be a small book-signing party at their Inman farm. They invited museum curators, cafe owners, B&B operators—the people they wrote about in the book. Even though it was a rainy, miserable day in November, more than a thousand folks showed up.

"We knew then that something must be done," said Marci who, with her dad, started the Kansas Sampler Foundation in 1993 for the sole purpose of preserving and sustaining rural culture.

To say their grassroots effort is working is an understatement.

Each year, the Kansas Sampler Foundation (along with dozens of Kansas communities) sponsors the Kansas Sampler Festival, an annual event that is best described as a living travel brochure. Representatives of rural communities all over Kansas show up to strut their stuff, to give Kansans a "taste" of all the great things to see and do in Kansas. There are covered wagon rides, threshing demonstrations, snake pits, and singing nuns, fifty strong. There are historical reenactors, folks like Amelia Earhart and Calamity Jane. There's Kansas cuisine—ostrich, verenike, bumbleberry pie, and alfalfa sprout enchiladas, to name a few.

Besides the festival, the Kansas Sampler Foundation sponsors the Kansas Explorers Club (see Northeast chapter), the We Kan! newsletter, the 8 Wonders Program, and the "Get Kansas" blog.

The Penner farm that was homesteaded by Marci's great-great-grandfather in 1874 is now home to a full-time Kansas Sampler Center. The hog shed, chicken house, barn, silo, and windmill have been replaced with a pond and deck, sixty varieties of Kansas trees and shrubs, flower gardens, and a reconstructed prairie. The grain elevator has been converted into a wood shop and Kansas display center, where Marci and Mil work like Kansas farmers during a drought to remind us of everything we have to be proud of.

To get the straight scoop from Mil and Marci, write them at the Kansas Sampler Center, 972 Arapaho Road, Inman, KS 67546, call (620) 585-2374, or log on to www.kansassampler.org.

★ ★

Pardon Me, but Your Slip Is Showing
Junction City

The Geary County Historical Museum just might host the most unusual fashion show on Earth. Called the Undercover Story, the fashion show features models wearing vintage women's underwear from the late 1800s up to World War I.

There are bloomers and petticoats, chemises and corsets. The models don't make Christy Turlington–size wages, and Victoria's Secret certainly hasn't been trying to lure them away. All of the Junction City models are volunteers, members of the local historical society, some of them eighty years old. Since Gaylynn Childs, the museum's director, came up with the idea in 1988, they've performed their not-so-risqué fashion show all over the state.

In the forty-minute show, each of the garments gets a little commentary as the husband of one of the models plays piano tunes from each item's era.

Unfortunately, the famous underwear (like a lot of my unfamous underwear) is getting fragile and doesn't travel well, so the museum has had to restrict the fashion shows to the museum itself at Sixth and Adams Streets in Junction City. Call (785) 238-1666 if you'd like a sneak preview, or log onto www.gchsweb.org.

One Man's Castle
Junction City

Retired algebra teacher Don Kracht had no idea he was building a medieval empire when he started digging a pond in the back of his Junction City lot. He just reckoned he'd transform the back two acres of his four-acre plot into a pond, since nothing seemed to grow there anyway. Heck, after three decades of teaching school, he figured he could use the scenery. But before he knew it, the pond had an island in the middle—and the island started looking deserted.

"I had the moat. I had the wooden drawbridge. I guess it wasn't too big of a leap to start thinking about a castle," Kracht says.

The Middle Ages in the middle of the county.
DON KRACHT

The proverbial castle in the air has been grounded.
DON KRACHT

★ ★

So in 1992, after staring at his island for four years, he began building a medieval castle, stone by agonizing stone. It might have ended up a small castle, except this crumbling rock house from the nineteenth century went on the market. Kracht picked it up for a song and began dismantling it and hauling it to the island.

"I was working on the castle and this woman comes by and asks, 'When did it start falling down?' I had to tell her it was going the other way," Kracht laughs.

Today, Kracht's castle is four stories tall and has towers, turrets, and a drawbridge. It even has a beer tap (in case he gets thirsty), a hot tub (should those stone-hauling muscles get sore), and a cannon (should warring kingdoms come calling).

Once a year, he throws a chislic party at the castle. Chislic is mutton on a stick that Kracht brings down from South Dakota and barbecues over a spit.

Castle Island is located off I-70 at exit 295, but if you want the official tour, call first. Don's number is (785) 238-3066.

Four Score and Twenty Years Ago
Lincoln

If you live in Lincoln, Kansas (population 1,262), you probably know that our sixteenth president didn't have a middle name, that he was every bit as honest as people claim, and that when he visited hospitals during the divisive Civil War, he visited wounded from both the Union and Confederate sides.

The reason you'd know this is because on February 12, Honest Abe's birthday, you probably got a Lincoln head penny for every question about Abe you answered correctly.

It's also likely that if you're a Lincoln native, you'd own a fake beard and a stovepipe hat. Because at high noon on the steps of the historic 1899 limestone county courthouse, there's a showdown between Abraham Lincoln look-alikes. Only one gets the honor of leading the freedom parade.

Will the real Abe Lincoln please stand up?

★ ★

The town, which indeed was named for our sixteenth president (a childhood friend from Kentucky moved here and helped settle the town), has been hosting a Lincoln Reenactment Day for more than twenty years.

Besides the Abe look-alike competition, there's a passionate reciting of the Gettysburg Address, a parade led by the local fife and drum corps, and a buffalo luncheon that used to cost exactly one picture of Abe ($5), but had to be raised due to the high price of buffalo meat.

If you do a "mean Abe" and feel like growing a beard, contact Marilyn Helmer at 139 West Lincoln Street, Lincoln, KS 67455; (785) 524-5133; www.villagelines.com. Lincoln is at the junction of Highways 18 and 14.

All Packed up and No Place to Go
Lincoln

In the Lincoln Cemetery on the east end of town, there's a gravestone shaped like a suitcase. It marks the grave of a nineteenth-century traveling salesman. His epitaph reads, "Here is where he stoped [sic] last."

Carved out of post rock limestone, the unusual headstone is living proof that the artist's rock-carving skills were superior to his spelling abilities.

The traveling salesman's name was J. S. Jacobs. In 1891, when he was only forty-two, he kicked the bucket while staying at Lincoln's old Windsor Hotel. Nobody could locate his relatives, so businessmen around town passed a hat and came up with the funds to honor the hardworking but family-less salesman.

It's a cute story. But it's not exactly true. Turns out old J. S. Jacobs was a traveling salesman, but he did not die without family. It's also doubtful he stayed at the Windsor. Why would he? His parents, Henry and Mary Jacobs, lived right in town. When they died in 1901, they were buried (albeit without suitcase gravestones) just north of J. S. in the same plot.

To pay your respects to either J. S. or the limestone suitcase, visit the Lincoln Cemetery at the east end of town on Highway18.

They Call the Show Messiah

Lindsborg

It's pretty easy to get posters of Miley Cyrus or Robert Pattinson. But have you tried to get a poster of George Frideric Handel lately? Not a simple task.

Unless you happen to be in Lindsborg, Kansas, where they sell a poster of his most enduring composition, *The Messiah,* which they've been performing for more than 120 years.

This little town of 3,000 hasn't missed an Easter season since 1882, when Alma Swensson, wife of Carl Swensson, the new pastor at the Bethany Lutheran Church, rounded up seventy-five local farmers, housewives, and shopkeepers to perform the famous musical that Handel wrote in 1741.

Reverend Carl saw *The Messiah* performed in Illinois and decided it would be a fitting musical for his newly formed Bethany Oratorio Society. So what if they didn't have a piano and had to use a tuning fork?

The chorus has grown a bit (there are now more than 300 volunteer singers and a fifty-piece orchestra) and improved a bit since that first choir of farmers and shopkeepers. In fact, the Bethany Oratorio Society has become so renowned that the performance has been nationally televised more than a few times, and the group has been invited to perform at Carnegie Hall.

To order tickets for the show, which takes place every Palm Sunday and Easter in Bethany College's 1,900-seat Presser Hall, call (785) 227-3380; www.bethanylb.edu.

★ ★

Castles in the Air

Lindsborg

Kansas is known for its flying houses. We have L. Frank Baum to thank for that. But the architectural wonder that many people have yet to become acquainted with is the Kansas castle. We have dozens of them. In Glen Elder, for example, there's a stone castle car wash. Sedan boasts the world's tiniest castle, although it has been locked in an abandoned building ever since Alyce Youngblood fell and broke her hip, forcing her to close the Lost Mine Confectionary. And in Wichita, there's a twenty-eight-room castle complete with a 300-year-old staircase imported from London. It doubles as a bed-and-breakfast.

But the most surprising castle is the three-tiered stone fortress that sits in the middle of nowhere. Well, it's not nowhere. It's in a twenty-six-acre park of wildflowers and native grasses 4 miles northwest of Lindsborg.

It's called Coronado Heights, and some folks might lead you to believe that Francisco Vásquez de Coronado, the famous Spanish explorer, built it when he came to Kansas looking for the seven cities of gold. Don't believe them.

Coronado did camp on the Smokey Hill Buttes where the castle is located, and he did write a glowing letter to the King of Spain describing Kansas as the best and most lush land he'd ever seen (not too surprising when you realize his search in 1541 only took him through Arizona, New Mexico, Texas, and Oklahoma). But alas, the castle was actually built in 1936 as a WPA project, along with outhouses and dams.

But no matter. There's a monument to Coronado at the castle, as well as a map of his North American trip, eighty-five winding steps, and picnic tables long enough to seat a reunion of Liz Taylor's husbands.

To picnic at the castle, take Highway 3 north out of Lindsborg to Winchester Road. Go west on Winchester about 4 miles until you see the park entrance. For more information, call the Lindsborg Chamber of Commerce at (785) 227-3706.

Follow the Dala Brick Road
Lindsborg

The Swedish Dala, an orange horse whose saddle and reins are painted with flowers, is a long-standing Lindsborg tradition. The Swedish town brought the horses from Dalarna, a Swedish province where they were first carved by lumberjacks for their kids.

Orange you glad I didn't say orange dala again?

★ ★

Lindsborg has been hanging them on porches and lampposts since the 1950s. I dare you to find three Lindsborg homes or businesses without at least one dala printed with either a last name or the traditional Swedish greeting, *Valkommen.* Even Lindsborg policemen have dalas on their badges.

A few years ago, the dalas got wind of the Chicago "Cows on Parade" and threw off their orange shackles. Ken Sjogren and Ken Swisher, owners of Heslojd, a Swedish import business, carved a 4-foot dala, stuck her in the back of a truck, and drove all around the country looking for fiberglass companies that could reproduce her.

Soon, Queen Kararina Ditto, as she's known, spawned Dalallama Telecomma, a dala with a third eye and telephone handsets, and Uppsa Dala Airways, a dala with wings, tail assembly, and electrically powered running lights. There's also Hello Dala, Salvador Dala, Dalalujah (which, of course, celebrates Lindsborg's tradition of singing *The Messiah*), Dalamatian, a firehouse dala with black and white spots, and Herd It Through the Grapevine, a dala with grapes and news items.

There are twenty-eight wild dalas, each of which was unveiled with a story, a song, and a cast of crazy characters—from the Flintstones to Mrs. Olsen and Juan Valdez. When Uppsa Dala Airways was unveiled, for example, airline peanuts and paper airplanes were passed out.

Lindsborg, planet of the dalas, is on US 81 south of Salina.

Oh, Give Me a Home Where the Sixty-one-ton Buffalo Roam
Longford

I've got some tragic news for the folks of Jamestown, North Dakota. You know that concrete buffalo you've been calling the world's largest? Well, it's not. There's a bigger one in Kansas.

It's not that we want to take away your glory. In fact, we wouldn't dream of advertising our buffalo. There are no signs. No brochures.

It's not even located on a main thoroughfare. Unless you follow the directions closely (and even then you'll probably stop a farmer to make sure), you'll never in a million years find it.

It's located on a 2,000-acre buffalo ranch at least 16 miles from the nearest interstate. It was built in 1978 by the ranch's owner, Ray O. Smith, and his brother, and if it makes you feel any better, Smith called his a "Smithalo," not a buffalo, and it got hit by lightning about the same time the governor and 3,000 Kansans showed up to dedicate it.

Smith, who died a few years ago, was a real character. His favorite comment was, "I'll tell you how smart the white man is. He killed off all the animals that could support themselves out here and replaced them with cows that need to be fed three times a day." He raised not only buffalo but lions, elk, and bear, too. For a while, he brought in extra income by putting one of his eighteen lions in people's laps and taking photos. Before Smith made the buffalo, he created a rock Christmas tree attached to a motor so it could spin in circles and a 37-foot concrete map of North America. He even hauled a rock from each of the fifty states and ten Canadian provinces to put in his geographic rock garden.

Our big buffalo is located on the highest rise on Smith's Circle 3 Ranch, which is now being run by Smith's son. From the 1,450-foot rise, you can see 40 miles. Next time I'm up there, I'll give the Jamestown buffalo a wave.

Nine Lives and Counting
McPherson

For years, linguists have attempted to trace the lineage of the "cats have nine lives" proverb. Egypt, the most likely candidate, bombed. Perhaps they should have come to McPherson where one cat, one very big cat, had at least nine lives.

His first life was as Leo, the MGM movie mascot that roars during

The Lion King.
BRETT WHITENACK AT MCPHERSON MUSEUM

opening credits. McPherson's Leo wasn't the first lion the vener-able movie company used. That was Slats, who is buried somewhere in New Jersey. The McPherson lion was the second Leo of six that have been chosen so far. His real name was Jackie, and while on a publicity tour for MGM under his assumed name of Leo, he sur-vived a plane crash in the Arizona desert and a boat sinking on the Mississippi.

He finally ended up in Kansas—or rather his hide did—in the 1930s after bank president Francis Vaniman added the Leo rug to his animal skin collection. After Vaniman died, his house became the local museum and his prize animal skins became the skeleton for the museum's African collection.

For a while, Leo was spread out on a black leather exam table, but museum guests kept plucking out bits of fur, so now he's under glass, soon to be in his own special downstairs case, according to museum curator, Brett Whitenack.

The McPherson Museum is located at 1130 East Euclid. Call (620) 241-8464 or visit www.mcphersonmuseum.com.

Trivia

What lion doesn't have an entourage? Leo's entourage includes a complete skeleton of a saber-tooth tiger, a giant ground sloth, a dire wolf, a collection of early bibles, and the first man-made diamond, created by a chemistry professor at McPherson College.

Car Bright, Car Light, First Car I See Tonight
McPherson

Jay Leno likes to joke that unlike most guys in Hollywood who have one car and thirty-six girlfriends, he has only one girlfriend (actually a wife, Mavis) and thirty-six cars.

And some of the cars in his three football-field-size warehouses near Burbank, California, have been worked on by antique auto restorers from McPherson, Kansas. Since 1997, the late-night host has provided a yearly full-ride scholarship, including tuition and room and board, to McPherson College's antique auto restoration program—the only program in the country that offers a college degree in the field of antique automobile restoration. But Leno, who also serves on the program's advisory board, isn't the only celebrity involved with the program. In past years, students have worked on cars owned by Nicholas Cage, Prince Ali Kahn, and Indy car driver John Hollandsworth.

The one-of-a-kind program has been around since 1976, when a McPherson oil tycoon couldn't find anyone to restore his extensive antique car collection. The program is often written about in *Popular Mechanics* and has been featured on the History Channel and, of course, *The Tonight Show* with Jay Leno. One student each year wins an internship to work at the Mercedes-Benz Classic Car Center in Fullbach, Germany.

The program is conducted at Templeton Hall at McPherson College. Call (800) 365-7402 for more information or visit www .mcpherson.ed/technology/.

Chim-chiminey
McPherson

If you grew up in the Midwest, it's quite likely that somewhere in your scrapbook is a parent-snapped photo of you and your siblings in front of a 36-foot-tall Happy Chef. At one time, there were more than fifty-six Happy Chef statues in seven Midwestern states. Kids dining at the once popular family restaurants could even push a button at the base of the three-story statue and hear a recorded message from the Happy Chef himself.

Unfortunately, most of the Happy Chef statues have been disassembled and sent to that big scrap heap in the sky. Except for the one in McPherson, where a former Happy Chef found himself in a whole new profession. Thanks to Vaughn Juhnke, owner of Chimney Specialists, the McPherson Happy Chef is now a chimney sweep wearing a top hat and a black tuxedo. And the spoon, well, it was replaced with a chimney sweep brush. The giant spoon, says Juhnke, won a coveted spot in the McPherson History Museum.

And while the Happy Chefs couldn't win any world's largest awards (after all, they were competing with fifty-five clones), Juhnke's chimney sweep is widely regarded as the world's largest. In 2002 when a local hooligan climbed up on the sweep and added a, well, let's just call it a "giant anatomy lesson," *Penthouse* magazine got wind of the prank and offered Juhnke $1,000 (he paid a mere $20 for the fiberglass chef) for a photo and story. Juhnke's foreman caught the added body part right away and took the papier-mâché digit down, but not before pictures of it circulated on the Internet. Juhnke wisely turned the magazine down, but his giant sweep sans anatomy lesson has made the comics in New York and a magazine in Germany.

Juhnke says that in some ways the Herculean chimney sweep has changed his life. "People come up to me in the store and shake my hand. They say, 'Thank you for rescuing the Happy Chef,'" he says.

The Chimney Specialists can be reached at 919 Seventeenth Avenue in McPherson (620-241-2869; www.chimneyspecialists.net). The sweep itself is just north of exit 54 on I-35.

The Stone Age
Minneapolis

In these days of million-dollar PR budgets, it's refreshing to find a genuine geological wonder without a concession stand. In fact, when you drive to Rock City, a national landmark with 200 huge rocks (some the size of a house) in the space of two football fields, you usually get lost. The signs are tiny, the roads are dirt, and you start

We built this city on rock, not roll.

to wonder what fool notion ever propelled you into wanting to see these sandstone concretions in the first place.

Until you arrive. Then you're just dumbstruck. How did these huge rocks get here? And furthermore, what in the heck are you supposed to do with them? You can't exactly skip them. You can't build houses out of them. About all you can do is name them after what they most resemble and then crawl on top. If you can make it.

But first, you have to deposit your $3 contribution in the rusted money box and sign your name in the guest book, a 39-cent note-book like the kind you used in second grade.

Once you've done that (and you'll probably be the only one there), you're free to wander around Turtle Rock, Kissing Lips, the Twin Sisters, and the other 197 monster rocks. When people say there's no place else on Earth like it, you'd better believe it. Because no one paid them to say it.

Rock City is 3.6 miles southwest of Minneapolis. Watch for the Rock City signs and bring binoculars.

"It Was Not Overly Pretty, But It Was Stout"
Morrowville

Lots of city parks have antique locomotives for kids to crawl on, but in Morrowville, the city park has a big red and silver bulldozer. I'm sorry to report you can't crawl on it (it's surrounded by a chain-link fence), but considering the fact that the world's first bulldozer was built right there in Morrowville in 1923, it's a small price to pay.

Farmer James Cummings was innocently watching his corn grow one day when he noticed the Sinclair Oil Company was having trouble laying pipes. Getting the pipes in the ground was no problem—newfangled technology took care of that. But to put the dirt back in the trenches, Sinclair workers relied on mules and dirt slips. Cummings wrote to the folks at the company and told them he had a better idea.

They cheered him on, and said, "Show us what ya got." Cummings wasted no time hooking up with J. Earl McLeod, a local

★ ★

draftsman. Scoring parts from local junkyards, they developed the
world's first bulldozer. So what if it was made from the frame of
a Model T, some old windmill springs, and other odds and ends?
It worked, or as McLeod said, "It was not overly pretty, but it was
stout." It was enough for the Sinclair Oil Company to award the rest
of the pipe contract—from Deshler, Nebraska, to Freemont, Missouri—to Cummings and McLeod.

A replica of the first bulldozer is located at Cummings Park on
Main Street.

Flour Power
Salina

Nancy Jo Leachman (see Chapter Six) divides her hobbies into two
categories. There's the OMG category where people see her kitschy
snow domes and say, "Oh my God, Herb, get in here. You gotta see
this." And then there's the quieter hobby of flour sack collecting,
where enthusiasts, usually older, sit down and want to tell you about
the mill where their father used to work or the underwear their mom
once made out of flour sacks.

"There's a real history to each one of my flour sacks," says Leachman, who at last count, had collected some eighty Kansas flour
sacks. "After I got divorced, I could live anywhere I wanted and I
chose to move to Kansas. I love wheat fields, and most of my flour
sacks, with a few exceptions, held wheat flour made at mills in towns
all over Kansas."

Between 1890 and 1929, flour mills sold their wares in fabric flour
sacks with art deco, silk screens, and other beautiful labels such as
Kiowa's State Line Milling company, which used a Kiowa Indian in
their logo.

"Before the invention of the sewing machine, flour was stored in
barrels," Leachman says, explaining that many of the logos are round
to fit on the top of a barrel. "The window of time for my collection is
very small, because after the Depression, flour mills, privvy to the fact

that people used flour sacks to make clothes after they finished with them, began selling flour in flower-print patterns. That's not what I collect."

What she does collect she finds in antiques stores, yard sales, flea markets, and occasionally on eBay.

Salina at one time, where she lives, milled more flour than any-where in the country.

"It's a very lonely hobby," she jokes. "They don't exactly have swamp meets for flour sacks."

No Special Sauce, Lettuce, Cheese—and Certainly No Sesame Seed Bun
Salina

Whatever you do, don't ask for cheese. The cook at Cozy Inn, a 12-foot hole in the wall that sells nothing but hamburgers, is apt to bonk you on the head with his greasy spatula. Not only would a slice of cheddar wreak havoc on his eighty-five-year-old gas-fired cast-iron griddle, but it would be a sacrilege to the institution of the Cozy, a 2½-inch burger that comes with catsup or mustard on a plain bun. Period.

The secret of these three-bite burgers is the onion. Each two-ounce ball is slathered with an onion mixture that's run through the meat grinder. You can't sit at one of the joint's six stools for even a minute without smelling like a Cozy for the rest of the day. And if you happen to order a few extra, do not—I repeat, do not—leave them in your car. Even Glade Super Fresh has its limitations.

For a while, nearby downtown businesses forbade employees to eat there. After all, they didn't want their businesses smelling like Cozy Inn. But now there's what the cooks call "the wimp window," so you can pick up a bagful to go without facing the curse of the permeated wardrobe.

Loyal customers run in and out, yelling, "Give me five" or "I need a dozen." A former governor of Kansas, who grew up in Salina, once ordered 500 Cozies for a staff meeting. Legends surround the place. A pregnant woman in troubled labor allegedly ate a bagful and her baby popped out. A man dying of heart failure requested one last meal of Cozies with all his siblings.

To grab a bagful, visit Cozy Inn at 108 North Seventh Street, (785) 825-2699, www.cozyburger.com. Just don't ask for cheese.

Hedge Funds
Scandia

If you want to make a class of second graders giggle, read them the assortment of names for a hedgeapple. The puckered, neon green fruit of the Osage orange tree (*Maclura pomifera*) has been called monkey brains, monkey balls, mock oranges, may apples, rootwood, naranjo chino, horse apples, brainfruit, greenbrain, and hedgeballs. Since you can't really eat them (they're not poisonous, but they're about as tasty as tree bark), making second graders laugh was about the only use for the prolific Kansas fruit.

That is, until Becki Neukirch-Carlson, a single mom from the tiny town of Scandia, acted on a well-known tenet of Marketing 101: "People will buy almost anything."

A friend dared her to put up a Web site selling monkey balls and, believe it or not, orders started rolling in.

"Oh, I ship them all over the country," she said. "People use them for decorations. I have one exotic florist in California who buys them by the case full."

Even Martha Stewart gave the ugly fruit a nod, running an article entitled "Enjoying Hedge Apples" in a Thanksgiving issue of her foofoo *Martha Stewart Living* magazine.

Although Neukirch-Carlson isn't allowed to post this on her Web site (in 2004 the EPA forced her to take it down), many folks swear by their pesticidal properties. Put one or two in the window well or behind the couch and you can kiss spiders, fleas, and other pests goodbye.

You Heard It Here First

Kansans tend to keep their inventions to themselves. They come up with things for their own amusement, not because they're hoping to mass-market them and eventually sell them to a big company like General Motors for $10 million. They make things because they need them and because they know they can.

Take Jule Lorenzen, for example. He used to live by himself in a schoolhouse outside of Galva, Kansas, that he rented for $15 a month. He liked to hang glide, and because Galva had a population of 664, most of whom are over age sixty, it wasn't exactly easy finding a tow—especially on a Tuesday afternoon when the wind is just right for making contact with thermals. So Lorenzen came up with a solution: He turned an old Honda 350 motor into a remote-control device that launched him and his glider into the air. Sans partner. He never marketed it. He made this unique remote-flying machine for his own enjoyment.

Every now and then, word of one of our Kansas inventions gets out and people come calling. Here are nine life-changing innovations that somehow managed to sneak out of Kansas:

1. The Slurpee

2. The time-release capsule

3. The bumper sticker

4. Mentholatum

5. The bulldozer

6. The Oh Henry! candy bar

7. The helicopter

8. The dial telephone

9. Autopilot

★ ★

"I had one guy claim they also keep mice away," she says. But don't expect to read that on her Web site.

Kansans have always known what to do with hedgewood—it makes termite-resistant fencepost, it puts on one heck of a spectacular light show when burned in a fireplace, and it even makes good guitars, mandolins, and bows.

Originally planted for fencing (farmers claimed hedge was "horse high, bull strong, and hot tight"), hedgerows became obsolete with the invention of barbed wire in the 1880s.

Orders for the resurging fruit can be placed on Neukirth-Carlson's Web site (www.osagehedgeballs.com) or by calling (785) 335-2619.

Harley, Come Home . . . and Don't Forget the Duct Tape
Scandia

When Richard and Sonia Raney opened Raney's Home Center, a hardware and home furnishings store in the tiny Swedish town of Scandia, they figured customers would flock for their custom wood cabinets, their extensive inventory, and their personalized customer service. Instead, customers come to dole out dog treats to Harley, their 65-pound yellow lab. Granted, Harley's no normal service dog. He rides to work on the back of Richard's Harley-Davidson, greets customers at the door, and retrieves duct tape, shims, WD-40, mousetraps, rags, and other items when customers request them. Perhaps his most impressive trick, something Lassie sure never did for Timmy, is opening the door to the pop machine and bringing cans of soda on command. At first, Richard and Sonia didn't want a *#@% dog, a Christmas present from their children, but Harley has become such an integral business partner that he even rides the forklift and attends KSU football games. Raney's Home Store, 205 Fourth Street, Scandia; (785) 335-2241; www.raneyshomecenter.com.

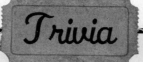

Trivia

In the 1870s, Kansans not only drove cattle to and from Texas, they drove wild turkeys, 5,000 of them, from Mitchell County to the railhead in Waterville, 60 miles away.

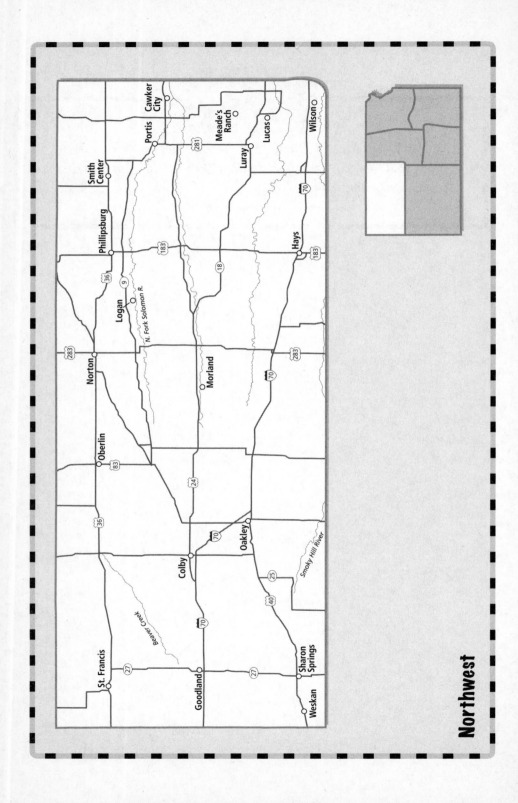

6

Northwest

In northwest Kansas, *practically every fourth person is a grassroots artist, an artist who takes whatever material is handy—tree trunks, old refrigerator doors, broken milk of magnesia bottles—and makes it into art. Other than Vincent van Gogh, who is represented by a three-story sunflower painting in Goodland, most of the artists from northwest Kansas make what the hoity-toity art world calls "outsider art."*

They paint, draw, sculpt, and put petrified shark's teeth in wax because "they have to." Because they're called by God, by angels, by unremitting dreams, or by a compelling need to express themselves.

Most of these artists have never heard of Monet or Matisse or their fellow northwest Kansas artist, van Gogh. Most, in fact, have little schooling of any kind. Inez Marshall, for example, was a truck driver before she started carving native Kansas limestone into motorcycles and life-size Abraham Lincolns. Lawrence Reynolds was a janitor, Leroy Wilson, a farmer.

There are also a lot of natural wonders in northwest Kansas, such as the Arikarae Breaks, a mini Grand Canyon near St. Francis, and Monument Rocks, 70-foot chalk walls near Oakley.

And when it comes to unnatural wonders, I dare anyone to try and top Cawker City's world's largest ball of twine.

★ ★

Goodness, Gracious, Great Balls of Twine
Cawker City

You can't grow up in Kansas without a flicker of pride for what used to be our only nationally known tourist attraction: the world's largest ball of twine in Cawker City.

This "king of string" weighs more than nine tons and would wind anybody who dared to run all the way around it. It's memorialized in downtown Cawker in an open-air gazebo. I've heard as many as 300,000 people come to see it each year. One couple from Salt Lake

Anyone got a REALLY big package that needs tying up?
LINDA B. CLOVER/CAWKER CITY'S BALL OF TWINE

City reported in the guest book that they'd driven nine hours out of their way for a once-in-a-lifetime photo op in front of the big ball.

But here's the problem. There are contenders for the title that Cawker City so proudly displays on signs leading into the city: WEL-COME TO CAWKER CITY, HOME OF THE WORLD'S LARGEST BALL OF TWINE. There's a ball of twine in Minnesota and one at Ripley's Believe It or Not! in Branson, Missouri, both of which claim to be larger.

All I know is that the Kansas ball keeps growing, thanks to Cawker City's annual Twine-a-Thon, which takes place the third Friday of every August.

The infamous tourist attraction was started by farmer Frank Stoeber, who allegedly tripped over some twine one day in 1953. In those days, hay bales were held together with twine, and the farmer had two choices: burn it or make it into a ball. Stoeber opted for the ball. Within four years, his ball of twine weighed 5,000 pounds and stood 8 feet tall. He continued to work on it until the state's centennial in 1961, when, feeling patriotic, he decided to donate it to the city.

If you want to be like Chevy Chase, who stopped to see the world's largest ball of twine in *National Lampoon's Vacation,* look for the open-air gazebo on the south side of Wisconsin Street (US 24) in beautiful downtown Cawker City. And if you call Linda Clover, who calls herself the Belle of the Ball, at (785) 781-4470, you can add twine at any time.

Where is Ball-do?
Cawker City

A little known art fact is that in the background of Leonardo da Vinci's famous *Mona Lisa* is the Rhine River. Well, if you go to Cawker City and look at its *Mona Lisa* (you can't miss it, it's right there in the old Basco Building), you'll see Waconda Lake, the nearest body of water to Cawker City. Look even closer and you'll see another Cawker City landmark, a rendition of the world's largest ball of twine. Mona herself is leaning on it.

We all scream for ice string?
LINDA B. CLOVER/CAWKER CITY'S BALL OF TWINE

In 2003, to celebrate the fiftieth anniversary of the great ball of twine, artist Cher Olsen painted forty of the world's most recognizable paintings, all featuring miniature versions of the now-famous orb—Cawker City's own *Where's Waldo?* There's Vincent van Gogh's *Starry Night* with the ball of twine as the sun, and Andy Warhol's famous soup can with the ball of twine instead of the soup label. In Edgar Degas's *The Dancers,* the twine ball is being kicked around on the wooden floor. Olsen even did a painting of the Statue of Liberty with the twine as the torch.

Although the paintings were all hauled out for the illustrious anniversary event (and are still there in the main drag's empty storefronts), Olsen started painting them two years earlier, after being transferred with her husband, Cawker City's Methodist minister, to the tiny town.

"I used to be an art teacher, but there weren't many jobs for art teachers in Cawker, so I came up with this project to keep from getting bored," Olsen says.

The community loved Olsen's paintings . . . except for one. Olsen's rendition of Michelangelo's *David,* with the twine ball covering his privates, had to be taken down after a local complained about the lack of propriety. The artist, after all, is the minister's wife.

Although you really can't miss them (they're placed in storefront windows along Cawker's Main Street), Olsen's paintings can be viewed from the "Twine Walk," a piece of twine painted on the sidewalk by a couple of high school kids.

Trapping Tourists
Cawker City

Brian Hodges, an avid roadtripper from Troy, Maine, claims there are five American landmarks that any sightseer worth his steel-belt Michelins simply must visit: Mount Rushmore, the Gateway Arch in St. Louis, Niagara Falls, the Grand Canyon, and, of course, the world's largest ball of twine.

★ ★

However, in his own quest to mark these must-see attractions off his list, he was shocked to discover nary a single souvenir shop in Cawker City. How was he going to prove to the "folks back home" that he'd really been to the ball of twine if he didn't have a postcard, a keychain, a beer mug, or a shot glass from the tourist destination?

Just when he was about to despair, Linda Clover, the self-appointed groundskeeper for the great ball, came to his rescue. She told him she'd seen Lottie Herod out watering her yard. All he had to do was stop by and Lottie would gladly open her Great Plains Art Gallery, an antiques store/souvenir shop with a working hand-cranked elevator.

Turns out Lottie, besides being a gardener, an antiques collector, and a souvenir stand operator, is an accomplished potter. She crafts teakettles, coffee mugs, salt-and-pepper shakers, and utensil holders all bearing the ball of twine's likeness. She also makes handmade postcards and made a handmade shot glass just for Brian when she heard he liked to collect them. She mailed it to him a couple years after his visit.

To say hello to Lottie or use her facilities, a bathroom wallpapered with the covers from old issues of the *Ladies Homes Journal,* visit her Great Plains Art & Antique Gallery at 719 Lake Drive (785-781-4344).

Trivia

Cawker City won its name in a poker game. Four friends—Huchell, Ride, Kshinka, and Colonel E. H. Cawker—played a rousing game of poker to see whose name would be plastered on the town's post office. Had they known then about the future ball of twine, perhaps Huchell, Ride, and Kshinka might have cheated more.

* *

The Great Pyramid of Colby
Colby

I think it's safe to say that Nellie Kuska of Colby wasn't fond of throwing things away. When she died in 1973, she had seventeen tons of possessions.

They weren't just any possessions, mind you. They were collections—big, big collections of dolls, toys, clocks, glass, ceramics, and furniture.

Several communities in California, where she was living at the time, wanted Nellie's collections. After all, Nellie, who even had her own radio show on the art of collecting, had rare dolls from Roosevelt's WPA program, a French fashion doll with a necklace of famous Louvre paintings, and a rare mechanical doll that blows kisses and waves. But no one in California was willing to take all seventeen tons.

When Kuska's three sons contacted the historical society in Colby, where she and her husband, agronomist Joseph Kuska, had lived for fifty years, they said, "Sure, bring it on down." Three moving vans later, the Prairie Museum of Art and History ended up with all 28,000 items, only 5 percent of which are on display. Even a twenty-four-acre site has limitations.

Nellie's collection is displayed in a three-story blue pyramid designed by her son, George Kuska, a California architect. It's next to a sod house, an old church, a one-room schoolhouse, and the largest barn in Kansas. Talk about open zoning.

The Prairie Museum of Art and History is at 1905 South Franklin Street, ¼ mile off I-70, exits 53 and 54. Phone (785) 460-4590 or visit www.prairiemuseum.org.

Van Gogh Lives Large
Goodland

You can't really miss a 24-by-32-foot painting, especially when it was painted by van Gogh and sits on an eight-story easel. Actually, the painting is a giant reproduction of one of seven paintings of sunflowers that van Gogh completed in Arles, France, in 1888 and 1889.

Easel-y the largest van Gogh reproduction in the United States.

SHERMAN COUNTY CONVENTION AND VISITORS BUREAU

Canadian artist Cameron Cross decided to reproduce those seven famous paintings, and he chose seven sites in seven countries that had a connection either to van Gogh or to sunflowers.

In Goodland's case, it has two sunflower processing plants, one of which produces oil for Pringles potato chips.

The painting's easel alone weighs 40,000 pounds and requires 30-foot-deep cement pilings just to hold it up. The painting weighs in at a mere 6,000 pounds. It took one and a half months and thousands of gallons of industrial-strength paint to create.

To go van Gogh, take I-70 to Goodland. You'll see Pioneer Park, where it's located, from the highway.

Now That's a Fish Story
Hays

In the 2000 presidential election, a fish in Barton County got 235 votes, only fifteen fewer than Ralph Nader. Of course, the fish wasn't just any fish. It was an 85-million-year-old fossil fish, a 14-foot sea monster that made Kansas famous in paleontology circles. The *Xiphactinus* fish, known as the X-fish, was one of hundreds that swam the great seas of Kansas back when Kansas was a sea.

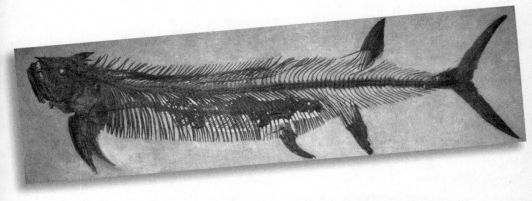

A bad case of indigestion!
FORT HAYS STATE UNIVERSITY'S STERNBERG MUSEUM OF NATURAL HISTORY

★ ★

Next to Sue, the *T. rex* that spawned a huge battle among the Feds, paleontologists, and private fossil hunters, an X-fish that sits in the Sternberg Museum of Natural History in Hays is the most famous fossil in the world. It's certainly the most photographed. Ask any paleontologist about the Gillicus in *Xiphactinus* (that means fish within a fish) and you'll get a knowing smile. It seems a 14-foot X-fish got a little greedy one day and tried to swallow a 6-foot cousin. Alas, it was the greedy fish's last meal. The cousin, a *Gillicus arcuatus,* thrashed so violently that it ripped the X-fish's insides to ribbons, killing it and causing it to sink into the paleontology record books.

George F. Sternberg, one of three brothers from a famous fossil-hunting family, found the rare fish-within-a-fish fossil 85 million years later. He excavated it in 1952.

The photogenic fossil is one of 3,750,000 artifacts in the Sternberg Museum, a 100,000-square-foot, four-story dome at 3000 Sternberg Drive. Phone (877) 332-1165 or visit www.fhsu.edu/sternberg.

Full Metal Racket
Hays

You can't call Lawrence Reynolds. He doesn't have a phone. Everything he needs to say is right there in his unique sculptures.

One of his scrap metal men trips over his tongue. The bottom reads, "Man is judged by the transgressions of his lips."

In another Reynolds sculpture, the Easter bunny is being crucified, the idea being that we've unjustly turned a religious holiday into a big commercial.

A man with deep convictions, Reynolds bases all of his work on verses from the Bible or sayings from popular culture. He worked as a recruiter for the Salvation Army before he moved to Hays, but he likes his janitor job at Fort Hays State University much better. With first dibs on the wood and old crates in the university's dumpsters, he plucks out two-by-fours and old shipping crates to carve into human figures.

Reynolds's rap on life.
STEVE SCHULTZ

Reynolds has also carved several trees in Buffalo Park, across from historic Fort Hays off US 183. Besides the park, his work can be viewed at the Grassroots Art Center in Lucas (213 South Main Street; 785-525-6118) and at Stone Gallery (785-625-7619) in Hays at 107½ West Sixth Street.

May the Horse Be with You

Hays

Like most grandparents, Marion and Donna Schmidt have scrapbooks of their eight grandkids. But they also have another, rather unique scrapbook—of their two dozen or so miniature horses. Those scrapbooks contain photos, records of registry, ribbons, and dozens of awards their horses have won in competitions.

The Schmidts' horses are tiny, some no bigger than a Great Dane. In fact to qualify as a miniature horse, the animal must be shorter

★ ★

than 34 inches at the withers. Miniature horses have been around at least since the seventeenth century, when Louis XIV bred them for his kids at the Palace of Versailles.

According to the Schmidts, who offer surrey rides and tours of their Blue Sky Farm, miniature horses are gentle, good with kids, and eat one-tenth what a full-size horse eats. In fact, many claim miniature horses are cheaper to feed than many large dogs.

The Blue Sky Farm is located at 1710 Canterbury Drive (785-625-6725; www.blueskyhorses.com).

Smithsonian West
Logan

Look on a list of Smithsonian's traveling exhibits schedule and you'll mostly see big cities, places like Miami and Chicago and Phoenix. But look again and you'll also notice the name of a little town in Kansas that you've probably never heard of, a tiny burg with a population of less than 600 that shows up on S.I.T.E.'s schedule several times most years.

Logan, Kansas, is anything but a popular travel destination. It doesn't even have a motel. But smack-dab in the middle of its 2-block downtown is the Dane G. Hansen Memorial Museum, a modern 10,000-square-foot museum that just happens to be one of the Smithsonian's best customers.

By the time it celebrated its twentieth anniversary, it had already hosted one hundred traveling exhibits from the venerable Washington, D.C., institution.

Thanks to Dane G. Hansen, an eccentric bachelor who slept until noon every day and who left the museum's foundation with $9 million when he died on his eighty-second birthday, the prosperous museum has been able to show Eskimo art, drawings by da Vinci, Japanese dolls, and moon rocks from NASA that Houston wouldn't loan unless a personal representative showed up to fetch them. Logan sent its mayor.

Hansen, an oil and construction magnate who sold mules to the U.S. Cavalry during World War I, lived in Logan his entire life. At one time his construction company employed 300, nearly half the town. He slept until noon every day because, as he said, "Nobody ever made a dollar in the morning. Mornings are for opening mail and answering phones." Instead, he worked until midnight, waking up colleagues all over the country with his late-night phone calls.

Polly Bales, former president of the museum association and wife of Dane's nephew, says while Dane would undoubtedly be proud of the memorial to his name, he'd probably question the budget for some of the exhibits.

Admission to the museum is free. It's open daily except Thanksgiving, Christmas, and New Year's Day, and can be found in Logan on Highway 9 between Speed and Densmore. Phone (785) 689-4846 or visit www.hansenmuseum.org.

Concrete Evidence
Lucas

When S. P. Dinsmoor was sixty-four, an age at which most people consider retirement, he launched an unusual career as an artist and social commentator.

Already he'd sired five children, raised two more stepchildren, served as a nurse in the Civil War, taught school, and farmed a small patch of property outside Lucas.

His real work, though, the work for which he's still remembered, began when he sold the farm and bought a half-acre plot of land in full view of the railroad tracks and only blocks from downtown Lucas.

The year was 1907. Dinsmoor, a staunch Populist, decided that just because the Populist party had gone down the tubes didn't mean its philosophy had to.

He spent the next twenty-one years espousing his mostly Populist views on religion, society, and monopolistic trusts in the only medium he could afford: concrete.

**With 113 tons of concrete and an overactive imagination,
you too can build your own Garden of Eden.**
JON BLUMB.COM

He started with an unusual eleven-room log cabin made out of
limestone logs. Giving tours, he used the admission fees to buy more
concrete—113 tons, in fact—which he used to sculpt concrete grape
arbors, American flags that swiveled on flagpoles, 40-foot trees, a
life-size Adam and Eve, a devil whose eyes light up (Dinsmoor was
the first in Logan to have electricity), and one hundred other statues.

His philosophy and humor were evident in everything he sculpted.
A carved concrete octopus representing monopolistic trusts had their
tentacles in bags of bonds, sacks of interest, the North Pole, and
the Panama Canal. He always said he used himself as the model for
Adam, a move that created quite a stir in Logan until he agreed to
add an apron to cover the statue's eyebrow-raising genitalia.

After Dinsmoor's first wife died, he married again when he was eighty-one. His wedding to twenty-year-old Emilie Brozek (who subsequently had two children with Dinsmoor) scandalized Lucas and brought even more publicity for his monument to modern masonry.

Dinsmoor called it the Garden of Eden and stipulated that when he died, he wanted his body placed in a glass-enclosed concrete coffin, so he could continue to keep an eye on admission-paying customers. He also sculpted an angel and a jug above the coffin. The angel, he said, was there in case he went up, the water jug in case he went the other way.

To view the work and the dead body of an unusual self-taught sculptor, a man some called the William Blake of the Wild, Wild West, visit the Garden of Eden in Lucas at the corner of Kansas and Second Streets (785-525-6395; www.garden-of-eden-lucas-ks.com).

Big Things in Small Packages
Lucas

I recently sent $20 to Erika Nelson so I could become an official member of her Museum of the World's Largest Collection of the World's Smallest Versions of the World's Largest Things. Erika, who lives in Lucas when she's not out rescuing small towns in her art car, is my hero. She's an artist, a visionary, and the world's foremost expert on the world's largest things. She has one of the top five coolest jobs in America.

Plus, by simply doing what she loves most, she is literally saving the world. In case you hadn't noticed, the choices in American cuisine are getting narrower by the day. So are the choices of retail establishments. These days, it's hard to tell if you're in Cleveland or Fort Lauderdale or Fremont, Nebraska, because they all have the same Wal-Marts, Pizza Huts, and Taco Bells. And some people think this is a good thing.

That's where Erika comes in. She has dedicated her life to one simple mission: "Combatting generica." That means she celebrates the

(Continued on page 213.)

But How Do I Cut My Sirloin?

Most towns with populations of 427 are lucky to have a gas station, let alone a museum. But Lucas, an anything but sleepy town in northwest Kansas, has five major museums, attracts scads of international visitors, and is definitely in contention for most interesting town in Kansas.

Especially if you like grassroots art. Also called folk art, outsider art, primitive art, and, yes, downright bizarre by some people, grassroots art thrives in Kansas—a state with more grassroots artists per capita than any other. And the Lucas Triangle, with its three vortexes of the Grassroots Art Center (a fascinating three-building museum with art made with everything from grapefruit peels and dried chewing gum to empty milk of magnesia bottles), the Garden of Eden, and the Deeble Rock Garden, is definitely the hotbed of grassroots art. To celebrate their grassroots heritage, the wacky folks of Lucas recently borrowed on the Chicago Cow idea and created unusual versions of giant "fork art," another name for grassroots art.

National Fork Producers Council?
STEVE SCHULTZ

Their most recent installation is Bowl Plaza, the world's largest toilet bowl. Created by several well-known Lucas artists, the big bowl has one tiny drawback. The stalls are so intricately designed (the women's side is mosaiced with female accoutrements, the men's side with masculine stuff) that people hog the bathrooms' glory while those outside in line suffer.

Now retired, the rolling museum hosts visitors on-site in Lucas.
ERIKA NELSON

one-of-a-kind, the kooky, the things that the rest of us tend to ignore or, worse yet, detonate. Erika reports that the folks in Sac City, Iowa, had the nerve to blow up their 2,225-pound popcorn ball.

Not only does Erika visit and take painstaking notes about each world's largest attraction, she makes her own tiny version that goes on display in either the Lucas museum, a converted senior citizen bus, or in Scout, the smallest art car in her fleet.

★ ★

The smallest version of the world's largest ball of rubber bands, for example, is made of those tiny rubber bands used on braces. The world's smallest version of the world's largest otter is made from a dachshund figurine and modeling clay. Other exhibits in her rolling museum are the world's smallest versions of the giant talking cow (made from an Elvis Presley valentine box), doughnuts, bats, eight balls, and badgers. The world's largest catsup bottle (which stands tall at 170 feet) stands 3 inches in Erika's museum.

Furthermore, after she creates the tiny knock-off, she returns to the original and shoots a photo of the big guy and its smaller clone.

For my $20 membership, I receive a full-year subscription to her newsletter, my own membership card, and a refrigerator magnet of one of the world's largest things. If I was even slightly wealthier, I would have signed up to be a Holstein ($35), because then I would have been awarded my own World's Largest Challenger Ball Starter Kit, which means that if I was dedicated enough, I could create my own world's largest ball of something and then Erika herself would come out, photograph it, and make a tiny version of it. Had I come in at the Pheasant member level ($100), I would have earned a blue paint chip from Babe, the Blue Ox in Bemidji, Minnesota.

Decisions, decisions.

Before Erika became the self-appointed curator of this unique museum, she was an art instructor at Kansas University. To contact Erika or view her museum, call (785) 760-0826, check out www.worldslargestthings.com, or write her at World's Largest Things, P.O. Box 101, Lucas, KS 67648-0101.

Think Pig
Lucas

Internationally acclaimed porcelain artist Eric Abraham says he always wanted to have a New York City loft and studio. In 2004, he bought one. In Lucas, Kansas.

Welcome to Eric's world.
ERIC ABRAHAM

"This studio fulfills my longtime desire to have a New York City loft. It's just that it doesn't have the hassles of New York City," Abraham says about the 6,000-square-foot Chevy dealership he recently converted into his Flying Pig Studio and Gallery.

The space includes a huge studio, a retail gallery, and a living space complete with a kitschen (yes, I spelled that right) that features 150 old radios.

Abraham has been making flying pigs since 1968, when an architecture student in his ceramics class at graduate school made thirty thrown piggy banks, much to the chagrin of the "serious art students." Abraham figured, "Well, if he can get away with it, so can I," and he concocted an unusual Mexican-style piggy bank mounted on a tall base with a Greek temple. He called it the *First National Oink*.

Abraham's ceramics (which have been featured on the *Today* show, the Discovery Channel, and HGTV) have only gotten wilder and crazier since then. Fairy tales are a popular theme, complete with fire-breathing dragons, hat-wearing pigs, and other whimsical creatures.

Abraham, who was born smack-dab in the middle of Harlem, has been making art since he was a kid, not a huge surprise since both his parents were artists who met while illustrating children's books for the public schools of New York City.

Flying Pig Studio and Gallery is located at 123 South Main, next to Brant's Market, purveyors of homemade Czech-style meats. Phone Eric at (785) 525-7722 or visit www.ericabraham.net.

Her Hobby Snowballed

Lucas

When Nancy Jo Leachman's daughter brought her a souvenir snow dome from a fourth grade field trip to Charlottesville, Virginia, she had no idea the beast she was unleashing. For the next several decades, the Salina reference librarian began collecting the little flake-filled souvenirs—also called snow globes and shakies—with an almost addiction-like passion. Although she finally moved on to other collectibles (see Chapter Five), she didn't stop until she'd amassed more than 2,000, 600 of which are on display in her Snow Dome Room of Meditation.

"These aren't the fancy ones with the glass domes and the wooden bases. These are the plastic souvenirs made in Hong Kong," Leachman says.

The kitschier, the better. Although her snow domes range from the Last Supper to Popeye, she's most proud of her Kansas snow domes that feature, among other things, the Greensburg well, Fort Leonard, Old Abilene Town, and Lucas, although the Lucas snow dome is one-of-a-kind, made for her by artist Tess McKnight to showcase her anomalous decision to buy a vacation home in Lucas.

"My sister who lives on Connecticut Avenue in D.C. laughs when I tell her I need to get out of the city," Leachman says of her Lucas vacation home where she retreats from the metropolis of Salina.

But where else would you open a Snow Dome Room of Meditation, a walk-in closet with a sixty-drawer card catalog filled with the tiny worlds of kitsch and wonder?

Although her daughter gave her the first snow dome, she's not "overly fond of the collection," Leachman says. "She made some disparaging comment about it the other day and I said, 'watch out, I'll leave it to your brother' and she retorted, 'Thank God.'"

The Snow Dome Room of Meditation can be viewed by calling Rossylyn Schultz at the Grassroots Arts Center or Connie Doherty at the Chamber (785-658-2211). Oh yeah, and Erika Nelson also has a key.

And You Thought Concrete Was for Bridges and Sidewalks
Lucas

Not 10 miles from Dinsmoor's Garden of Eden, another unknown artist was also busy casting concrete. This artist, Ed Root, didn't do it to make his political or religious views known. He did it because he broke his hip in a car accident and could no longer farm the family homestead or make illegal moonshine. Until the Kansas Grassroots Art Association discovered him, it's doubtful anybody but his wife and ten kids ever saw the magnificent work he created by casting concrete and then embedding it with shards of glass and pottery, Milk of Magnesia bottles, plastic toys, screw-in fuses, perm rods, buttons, and anything else he could find. After his wife died, he even

★ ★

used the family china. When the grandkids came to visit, he'd hand them five-gallon buckets and instruct them not to come back until they'd filled them up.

He made hundreds of concrete pieces, ranging from three-tier birdhouses and 7-foot tomblike creations to small doorstops with rabbits, which he showcased in the family home, along with rambling collages of foil, crepe paper, and paper flowers.

When the Army Corps of Engineers decided to turn Root's property into Wilson Lake, Root went after them with a shotgun. But in 1960, when he was ninety-four, he finally died and the Army flooded his land.

The good news is the Grassroots Art Center still has hundreds of Root's pieces on display at 213 South Main Street. Phone (785) 525-6118.

Postcards from the Edge
Lucas

Florence Deeble was just a punk kid when S. P. Dinsmoor was constructing his lavish, nationally known Garden of Eden. Although she enjoyed walking by his house, she didn't fancy herself a wannabe. Rather, she aspired to teach English and history, which she did for forty-two years.

But in 1951, after a kid in nearby Osborne fell into a fish pond and drowned, her mom asked her to fill in the family's backyard fish pond with concrete. It was a moment of destiny.

First, she added a bit of color, a few rocks. Uh-oh. Florence was hooked. She soon began creating concrete postcards of all the places she visited. An avid traveler, she made postcards of Mount Rushmore; the Grand Tetons; Arizona deserts; Shiprock, New Mexico; Colorado's Long's Peak; and Estes Park, where she owned a cabin and spent her summers. When she was no longer able to travel, she concentrated her efforts on Mount Lucas with Mount Rushmore–like heads of Lucas dignitaries. The Lucas city band was prominently featured.

* *

Until her death in 1999 (she was six months away from turning one hundred), she led tours of her rock garden dressed in heels and turquoise jewelry.

"I like to garden—to rock garden," is how she explained it.

Deeble's Rock Garden can be viewed at 122 Fairview Street. For more information, call the Grassroots Art Museum at (785) 525-6118.

South Dakota? Who needs South Dakota?
STEVE SCHULTZ

★ ★

But Where's Ken?

Lucas

The Garden of Isis, inside the old Florence Deeble house, is not the place to plan a birthday party for five-year-olds. At that age, party-goers still have a tendency to put Barbie (you know, that plastic doll with the 36-24-36 figure) on a pedestal. They like to dress her like a prom queen or a bride or a candy striper and hope that someday they'll grow up to be just like her.

They might not look too kindly on the fact that Mri Pilar has created a whole art installation from discarded Barbie dolls. She calls

Tinfoiled again.
STEVE SCHULTZ

them Rebarbs and, yes, some of them have been dismembered, reassembled, and given butch haircuts.

Not that Pilar has a personal vendetta against Barbie. Well, maybe she's a tad bit put off by Barbie's role as an icon of perfect womanhood. She just likes taking things that people no longer see a use for and turning them into art. She's nothing if not democratic in her choice of art materials. Besides Rebarbs, the five-room Garden of Isis features clocks, hair barrettes, kitchen utensils, car parts, computer motherboards, plastic dinosaurs, and anything else Pilar can scrounge from the recycle bin.

All of the walls and ceilings of this 1906 home are covered in foil and silver insulation. There's not a single square inch that hasn't been transformed into an art assemblage, all woven together by Slinkys. Besides the Rebarbs, Pilar's installation features lots of unclocks (that's a clock that no longer keeps time), an Isis Chapel, and an Isis Grotto.

Viewing of the Garden of Isis is included in the admission fee for the Grassroots Art Museum. The Garden of Isis is located a few blocks away at 213 South Main Street. Call (785) 525-6118 for more information.

Quilted Basement

Luray

From the street, Leroy Wilson's house in Luray looked like every other house on his block—beige, middle-class, relatively boring.

But, boy oh boy, open the door to the basement and you'd fall headfirst into Alice in Wonderland's rabbit hole.

Leroy, who retired from farming after an unfortunate car wreck, painted every door, wall, water pipe, phone line, furnace, and gas valve in the family basement. And when that was finished, he painted over it and started again. For twelve years until his death in 1991, he did little but paint wild triangles, mosaics, and quilting patterns on every square millimeter of the family basement.

Neighbors used to drop off leftover paint. His wife, who wasn't crazy about his new hobby, refused to let him touch anything upstairs.

In fact, a former tenant of one of Wilson's rental houses reported that the insides of the kitchen cabinets were painted with Wilson's mosaics. Thankfully, his wife didn't bother to open the cabinets, so she never caught on.

Although the basement was painted over when the Wilson house was sold, a cabinet and pieces of the wall have been preserved at the Grassroots Art Center in Lucas, 213 South Main Street, (785) 525-6118.

A Pin through the Heart of America
Meade's Ranch

In 1918, the United States Coast and Geodetic Survey took a piece of cardboard, cut out the shape of the lower forty-eight states, and balanced it on a pinpoint. This center of the United States (39¼° 50′ N latitude, 98¼° 35′ W longitude, to be exact) just happened to fall in the middle of a hog farm near Lebanon, Kansas. The locally run Hub Club, assuming this designation could lead to considerable tourist revenue, ceremoniously installed a pyramidal stone monument with a brass plaque on a hilltop just outside of town. Inscribed with a bold declaration—THE GEOGRAPHIC CENTER OF THE UNITED STATES—the plaque wasn't exactly correct. The farm was three quarters of a mile away, but hog farmer Johnny Grib wasn't too keen on turning his beloved farm into a tourist trap. Especially when the state government got involved, ponying up the money for a hotel and road crews to pave a 1-mile strip leading to the site.

Unfortunately, the great hordes of tourists never arrived, and the hotel was sold to Texas investors who only visit once a year during hunting season.

Forty-two miles south of Lebanon, another sign and plaque announce yet another center, THE GEODETIC CENTER OF NORTH AMERICA.

Center of the universe.
JAMES S. DICK

This sign makes no claims at being the geodetic center itself; rather it indicates that the real geodetic center lies on private property 8 miles away at Meade's Ranch, which is also marked with a small bronze geodetic survey marker.

Every calculation of latitude or longitude anywhere in North America uses this base on Meade's Ranch as the starting point. Anytime a surveyor between Mexico and Canada checks property lines using geodetic markers, he's positioning that property in relationship to a ranch in Kansas.

★ ★

Holy Guacamole, Batman, What Are We Doing in a Bank?
Morland

Would-be robbers beware! In Morland, a little town of 165, the local
bank boasts its very own collection of superheroes.

Morland's Citizen's State Bank doubles as a comic book museum,
with 164 comic books on display.

Once belonging to local Morland boy Floyd Riggs, the collection
was uncovered by Floyd's mom after he died of cancer at age forty-
two. Carefully bundled in old lard cans, the colorful collection, which
includes the Lone Ranger, Tarzan, Lassie, and other popular comics
from the '40s and '50s, was carefully mounted and framed. For a
while, thanks to the prompting of a local art teacher who recognized
the collection's value, it toured the state as a traveling art exhibition.

To see the Floyd Riggs comic book collection, visit the bank at 511
West Main Street. The bank also has a brick mural of all the flora and
fauna unearthed in the local fossil dig funded by the National Geographic Society in 1985 and 1986. Phone (785) 627-3165.

Hail to the Losers
Norton

On January 22, 2009, when the rest of the country was celebrating
Barack Obama's inauguration, Lee Ann Shearer, the curator of Norton's Gallery of Also-Rans, inaugurated a 16 x 20 black and white
photograph of John McCain.

While McCain's name is still a household word, try these on for
size: Winfield Hancock, Rufus King, or De Witt Clinton? These men,
powerful and famous during their lifetimes, are victims of a well-
known political rule of thumb: The winner in presidential elections
gets the White House; the loser gets doomed to obscurity.

De Witt Clinton, for example, was a mover and shaker who
launched the Erie Canal and swept the Republican nomination in
1812. But thank to James Madison, the Democrat who defeated him,
his name can barely be recalled.

★ ★

That's not the case in Norton, Kansas, where presidential losers get their glory at the Gallery of Also-Rans. Housed in the mezzanine of Norton's First State Bank, this little museum was even more obscure than its subjects, hosting thirty or so visitors a year, until *USA Today* got wind of it. Sparked by the Bush-Gore election, the outcome of which held the country's attention for thirty-seven long days after votes were cast, this museum suddenly took on a new importance.

W. W. Rouse, former president of the bank, started the museum in 1965, after one of his daughters gave him a book by Irving Stone called *They Also Ran.* A history buff who loved lively political debate, Rouse was particularly intrigued by Horace Greeley, who lost to Ulysses S. Grant in 1872. He decided the losers, too, needed a tribute, and he began collecting pictures of them. Until his death in 1981, Rouse wrote to the Library of Congress every four years requesting a photo. He also wrote the commentary about each candidate, and his colorful personality is apparent in every entry.

Now Shearer serves as curator, commentary writer, and tour guide for all who come to see the ones history eventually leaves behind.

The Gallery of Also-Rans is at the First State Bank at 105 West Main Street in Norton. Call (785) 877-3341.

Prairie Dog Companion
Oakley

When *National Geographic* ran its April 1998 cover story on the plight of the prairie dog, it's no big surprise they didn't rush to Prairie Dog Town outside Oakley. Granted, this tourist trap has a native habitat of the burrowing animals that live in huge communities across the western prairies, but the prize attraction, and the one that brings in the tourists by the carloads, is an 8,000-pound prairie dog, the largest in the entire known universe. Or at least that's what the billboards on I-70 proclaim. So what if it's made of concrete and its face is starting to weather in the strong Kansas winds?

★ ★

This cheesy tourist attraction also features a live five-legged cow, a dead two-headed calf (it's stuffed and encased in glass, thank goodness), a petting zoo, and rattlesnakes.

P. T. Barnum would have felt right at home.

To pet the freak bovines or have your picture taken with the "big dog," stop by Prairie Dog Town at 457 US 83, off I-70, near the Oakley exit, or call (785) 672-3100.

The Show Must Go On
Oakley

In 2001, when the owners of the Palace Theatre were forced to shutter the one entertainment venue left in Oakley, "We just looked at each other and thought, 'Now what?'" says Nicole Keenan, who was in high school at the time. "We didn't have anywhere to go."

And it didn't take long to show.

"Mischief skyrocketed," says Oakley Chief of Police Dan Shanks. "Our kids had nothing to do."

Community leaders put their heads together and hatched an innovative plan to kill two birds with one stone. They'd reopen the theater as a nonprofit with high school kids running the show.

"The students do everything from keeping the books, writing the checks, and paying the bills to recruiting volunteers for the concession stand," says Jim Keenan, the high school business teacher who developed the yearlong entrepreneurship curriculum.

Their idea was a smashing success: Teen crime is down as crowds of 250 pack the house on weekends. The Palace prices rock: $5 tickets and $3.50 for snacks and a drink.

"This has been one of the best things I've seen this community do," says moviegoer Barb Glover. "It gives parents a safe place to drop off their kids. It keeps teens off the highway. But more importantly, it gives these teenagers real life experience in running a business."

Indeed, Taylor Ellegood, one of six students who ran the theater in 2009, says, "It's not very often you find a job that gives you all this real world experience. After a year of doing this, I could easily go out and start my own business. Plus, I've learned how not to flip out when customers get upset." To catch a flick, stop by 101 Center Avenue, Oakley; (785) 672-3115; www.palacetheatreoakley.com.

Teeth for Two
Oakley

One day back in 1964, Viola Fick looked down at the ground on her ranch near Monument Rock and saw seventy-two fossils of sharks' teeth. She and her husband, Earnest, borrowed what Vi called "a learner's book on fossils" from Earnie's nephew, who was attending Fort Hays State University, and began to search in earnest. Before it was all said and done, the amateur paleontologists found thousands of Cretaceous fossils, including 11,000 fossilized sharks' teeth, all within 50 miles of Oakley.

After a while, the sharks' teeth started looking the same, so Vi did what any sensible person would do—she started turning them into art. She made eagles, American flags, the Presidential Seal, the State Seal of Kansas, and, of course, a bas-relief sculpture of a shark—all out of shark's teeth. One of the eagles had a snake in its talons, but she used rattlesnake rattlers for that. Her best sharks' teeth were reserved for embedding in the fancy frames she made to show off her portraits of flowers, trees, and people, all made with melted wax, papier-mâché, paint, glue, and fossils.

As one of the curators at the Fick Fossil Museum said, "They didn't have cable back then."

Vi's final body of work includes hundreds of artworks from fossilized sharks' teeth, vertebrae, fish jaws, shells, and crinoids.

The museum, which shares space with the Oakley Public Library, is located at 700 West Third Street. Phone (785) 672-4839 or visit www.discoveroakley.com.

★ ★

Cinderella Story
Oberlin

In an age where fitness centers vie for the hottest new workout equipment, LandMark Inn, an historic Oberlin bank turned B&B, is an oddity. Owner Gary Anderson bids on the oldest, out-of-date workout equipment he can find, dinosaurs really from the turn of the century. He uses the antique workout equipment to stock the Historic Registered Inn's

Do they teach Pilates?
JAMES S. DICK

vintage gym. Among other things, he landed an 1866 rowing machine, an antique cedar sauna, and an 1886 stationary bicycle. The LandMark's gym is so authentic that when director Ron Howard filmed *Cinderella Man,* the period movie about boxer James Braddock's 1930s comeback, he went straight to Gary Anderson, begging to rent out most of his gym. LandMark Inn also has an old-time mercantile, Teller Restaurant, and seven suites with carved beds, ornate wallpaper, arched pine windows, Victorian sinks, and original pictures of Buffalo Bill Cody, who may or may not have worked out on the stationary bike. The LandMark Inn is at 189 South Penn, (785) 475-2340; www.landmarkinn.com.

Who Needs a River?

Phillipsburg

At last count, there were 9,485 American towns with annual river festivals. You know, those summer festivities where antique fire trucks parade through downtown, kids smear cotton candy on their spankin' new rompers, and old-timers reminisce about "the good ole days." Most of these towns come by their river festivals honestly, which is to say, there's an actual river running through town.

Phillipsburg, a county seat on US 36, didn't consider the fact that their closest river is an entire county away to be a hindrance. Heck, in a move that undoubtedly ranks in the Final Four of Turning Lemons into Lemonade, Phillipsburg turned their lack of river into a cause for celebration. Every year since 1984, the Phillipsburg Area Chamber of Commerce throws an annual festival, complete with turtle races, arts and crafts booths, a car and motorcycle show, and more than 20,000 revelers who show up each year to chow down on Phillipsburgers, a local hamburger drenched in a secret sauce found only in Phillips County. And as for watering holes, Phillipsburg does have a swimming pool, admission for which is completely free during the tongue-in-cheek festival, going strong now for more than twenty-five years.

For more info, contact Phillipsburg Area Chamber of Commerce, 270 State Street, Phillipsburg, (785) 543-2321.

★ ★

Trivia

Twenty miles south of Oakley, off a dirt road on a private ranch, are 70-foot towering chalk walls and turrets. They're called Monument Rocks, and the owners don't mind people visiting the nationally designated landmark, but they don't appreciate climbers. It's 20 miles south of the junction of US 40 and US 83, then 7½ miles east and south on Jayhawk Road.

From Limestone to Limelight

Portis

Back when Inez Marshall was giving personal forty-minute tours of her Continental Sculpture Hall, she used to tell her guests, "It's the only one of its kind in the world."

She was not exaggerating. For fifty years, the former truck driver, auto mechanic, and traveling evangelist sculpted Model Ts, churches, log cabins, and just about anything else you can think of out of native Kansas limestone. The Model T, which weighs 600 pounds, has a motor, a transmission, U-joints, a drive shaft, a radiator, and headlights and taillights that still work.

In the full-size dining room scene she sculpted of Abraham Lincoln and his family, Abe alone weighed 500 pounds. Even though she was partially disabled, Marshall managed to turn monstrous and very heavy pieces of limestone into the Lord's Supper, a Kennedy table (a tribute to JFK, it had dozens of Kennedy dollars embedded in it), and an eleven-room Sunshine Hospital that had doctors, an operating room, a nursery, and a dining hall complete with food on the tables.

After lying in bed for a year and a half (she'd broken her back while hauling corn to Kansas from Iowa), Inez suddenly felt the urge to get up and go to the door. She immediately was drawn to a small rock. She said to her dad, "Hand me that rock."

He did.

"Now, hand me a knife."

Again, he heeded her request.

Even though she'd never shown even the slightest inclination toward carving, she immediately sculpted a cute little squirrel with its tail standing up. Within a few months, she'd made dozens of small rock sculptures.

Her dad ran an ad in the back of a magazine and before she knew it, she was carving limestone salt and pepper shakers of hundreds of species of birds. A pair of scarlet tanagers or orange-crowned warblers, for example, sold for $1. Soon, she had so many commissions she couldn't keep up with them.

Besides, bigger projects were beckoning. In the 1960s and '70s, she opened the Continental Sculpture Hall, first in Abilene and then in an old gas station in her hometown of Portis. She gave tours wearing her signature red cap and blue sweater.

After she died in 1984, a dentist from Florida snatched up most of her work, but now it's back in Kansas. You can see ninety-five of her pieces at the Grassroots Art Center at 213 South Main Street in Lucas.

Snake, Rattle, and Roll
Sharon Springs

When I see a snake, I scream bloody murder. When women in Sharon Springs see snakes, they think, "Wow! What a great idea for a festival." Or they did.

Of course, the five women who launched the Sharon Springs Rattlesnake Roundup were used to seeing snakes, big prairie rattlers that slither rampantly in this part of the state.

Snakes, in fact, are a lot more rampant than tourists, who tend to avoid this little burg that's a good 30 miles south of I-70. After the sugar beet industry went belly up in the 1980s, the traffic in Sharon

Custer's First Stand

Everybody knows about the Battle of Little Big Horn, the infamous battle where General Custer lost his life. But the twelve-year Plains War that culminated on that famous Montana battlefield actually started in northwestern Kansas when on November 29, 1864, a tribe of Cheyenne men, women, and children were brutally massacred in their camp on Sand Creek in Colorado. Survivors made their way to Cherry Creek near St. Francis, Kansas, and began passing the war pipe. Nearly 3,000 Indians from many tribes came to declare war on the white man who was destroying their people. On New Year's Day 1865, they set out to get their revenge.

The Dog Soldier Monument at the Cherry Creek Encampment site stands as a memorial to the Cheyenne who died at Sand Creek. The monument, by Cheyenne county historian and metal sculptor Tobe Zweygardt, features a metal tepee guarded by an Indian brave astride his horse atop a nearby bluff. It is located north of St. Francis on Highway 27.

Sign, sign, everywhere a sign.
JAMES S. DICK

Springs dried up almost completely, except for the few mountain climbers who traipsed there to climb Mount Sunflower, the highest point in Kansas.

Judie Withers and four of her friends started pondering what they had to offer.

"We didn't have much except snakes. Lord, did we have snakes," Judie says.

The five women proposed a rattlesnake roundup, testified in Topeka to make it legal, and hosted the event ever since. Talk about killing two snakes with one stone.

Thousands trooped to Sharon Springs to eat rattlesnake meat, view the 12-by-24-foot rattlesnake pit, and watch Fangs and Rattlers, a touring exhibition team that performed such tricks as stuffing twelve live rattlers into a sleeping bag with a live man in it.

A $100 prize and a trophy went to the rattlesnake wrangler who brings in the biggest snake. The record is 53½ inches. The festival was held Mother's Day weekend each year.

Into Thick Air
Weskan

Mount Sunflower, the highest point in Kansas, used to have a cow skull sitting on it. Now it has a giant sunflower made of railroad spikes, a mailbox, and a plaque that says nothing happened here in 1897.

Still, mountain climbers from around the country troop here to mark its 4,039-foot elevation off their list.

For some low-altitude mountaineering, visit Sunflower, mountain of doom, just ½ mile east of the Colorado border. Go 3 miles west on US 40, 11 miles north on a gravel road, then 0.9 mile west and you should see a sign at the pasture gate. Three-tenths of a mile later, after crossing the cattle guard, you'll reach the summit. If you'd like a native guide for your mountaineering expedition, call Ed Harold at (785) 943-5444. He's the guy who owns the private property and who made the marker.

Grand Canyon of Kansas

Ten miles north of St. Francis, the yucca-covered high plains suddenly drop off into a breath-taking canyon sculpted out of 9,000-year-old loess hills. This 36-mile Grand Canyon of the Plains that stretches into Nebraska is called the Arikaree Breaks, and if it were located anywhere else, tourists would flock and buses would be dispatched. As it is now, it's accessed by a potholed dirt road with numbered red metal disks that correspond to a tiny blue brochure that can be picked up at the Hilltop General Store.

As flat as Dolly Parton.
JAMES S. DICK

Winning Isn't Everything, but It Sure Ain't Bad

New York Times reporter Joe Drape spent the fall of 2008 in Smith Center covering the high school football team that hasn't lost a game in eight seasons. At Hubbard Stadium, locals duct tape their blankets to the bleachers the night before to save seats. Every morning from 8 to 9, a group of men, mostly senior citizens, hook up at the Second Cup Cafe. They call themselves "As the Bladder Fills," and their shenanigans are detailed every week in the *Echo,* a four-page, typewritten newspaper that former mail carrier Ivan Burgess writes and distributes through his Last Legs Publishing. He reports on jokes and local news and provides vital definitions of such Smith Center pastimes as bingo. (It's when one little old lady yelling "bingo" makes fifty little old ladies say, "damn.")

Talk About Going Round and Round
Wilson

If the prisoners in *Midnight Express,* the 1978 movie about American college kids thrown into a Turkish prison, had been captured in Wilson, they'd have no choice but to walk in circles, an activity that many of the prisoners in the movie undertook once they lost their minds. The Wilson City Jail, a tiny two-story native limestone structure with a tin roof, is round. Until 1912, it was used as the city water tower. When the newfangled water tower went in, the round stone building took on a new life. But unlike the Turkish prisons, the prisoners here couldn't stay much longer than eight hours. It didn't have a bathroom, and the

★ ★

sheriff had to transfer them to Ellsworth, the county seat, the next morning.

The historic round jail is located a half block off Main Street on E Street, just past the railroad tracks.

Giving prisoners the runaround.

Southwest

Get out your *Kleenex. There was no Matt Dillon. At least not in Dodge City. The famous Gunsmoke character was a composite of many famous lawmakers who tried (most of the time unsuccessfully) to main-tain order in the town that between 1872 and 1885 was called every-thing from "hell on the plain" to "the wickedest city in America."*

Wyatt Earp and Bat Masterson are just two of the real marshals who tried to keep an eye on all the buffalo hunters, cavalry soldiers, and cowboys who drove herds of longhorns right down the main street of Dodge. Indian territory was 10 miles west of town, and Boot Hill Cem-etery (where scores of men were buried with their boots on) was right on the main drag.

For the most part, the Wild West has been tamed, but in southwest Kansas, there's still a lot of wild (and crazy) goings-on: wild animals (elephants who take baths in public swimming pools), wild businesses (a wildly successful dot-com that sells tumbleweeds), and artists using wild media (Pizza Hut boxes, for starters). Desperadoes still roam the plains, like Perry Smith and Richard Hickock, who shocked the world in 1959 and even lured Truman Capote out of New York to research In Cold Blood, *and M. T. Liggett, who is doing everything he can to kill any vestige of conventionality. Well, read on. You'll see.*

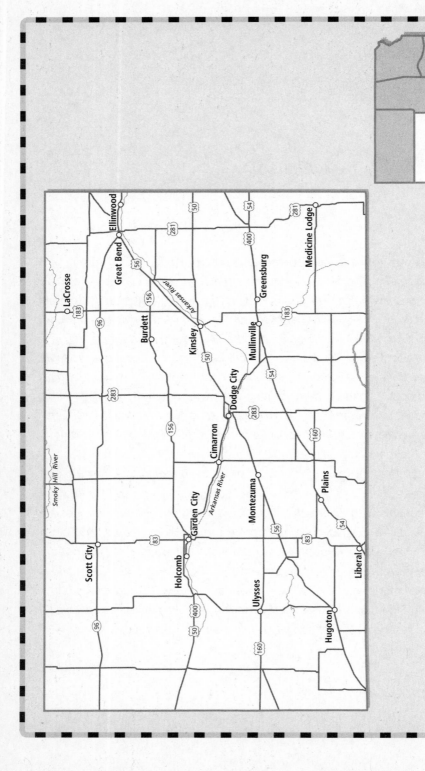

★ ★

Of Course Pluto's Different—It Was Discovered by a Kansan

Burdett

Back in 2006, some astronomers with a bee in their bonnet decided to create a stir. What with no new planets having been discovered in seventy-six years, they started getting antsy and decided the astronomy circle needed shaking up. They started arguing that Pluto, the ninth planet, should be downgraded to a dwarf planet. Pluto, they insisted, was too puny, had an eccentric orbit, was solid rather than gaseous like the rest of the planets, and hadn't knocked other stuff out of its orbital neighborhood.

Unfortunately for Burdett, Kansas, the International Astronomical Union decided to rearrange all those science teachers' charts. Technically, Pluto is still a planet, but it's only a dwarf. Still, this little town of 241 has kept the sign on the west edge of town, the sign that tells about Clyde Tombaugh, the local kid who discovered Pluto—the only planet discovered by an American—on February 18, 1930.

When Clyde was just a kid, he built a 9-inch telescope from junk farm machinery and a shaft out of his father's 1910 Buick. At age twenty-two, he wrote to the Lowell Observatory in Arizona, figuring experts there could explain some of the questions his high school instructors couldn't answer.

Those experts were so impressed with Tombaugh that they wrote him back and offered him a job. Two years later, when he was a still-wet-behind-the-ears twenty-four, he found Pluto.

As he once said, "It was better than pitching hay on my father's farm."

The plaque honoring Tombaugh is west of Burdett on Highway 156. If you'd rather look at some stars in his honor, call the Clyde W. Tombaugh Observatory at the University of Kansas in Lawrence at (785) 864-3166.

How Wheat It Is To Be Loved by You

Cimarron

Wheat germ, swheat germ! Far be it from me to knock wheat germ. I have no qualms with nutritionists who claim wheat germ has more fiber than cardboard, more protein than an eighty-two-ounce T-bone. All I'm saying is why bother with something that sounds contagious when you could just as easily lace all your breads, salads, and cereals with wheat nubs instead? Wheat nubs, a crunchy alternative to wheat germ, are just as nutritious, just as fiber packed, and they come in thirteen flavors.

They're also just one of dozens of healthy wheat products created by home economist Shirley Voran at her Kansas Wheat House, a one-of-a-kind business on the main street of Cimarron. Take S'wheat Hearts, for example, a delicious wheat-centered, chocolate-dipped candy that was a smash a few years ago at Bloomingdale's. Or S'Wheat Heart Roses, wheat-based roses that taste like a Cherry Mash and come with a poem.

When Voran was a kid helping her dad transport the family wheat harvest to the grain elevator, she always wondered, "Why do we have to sell our wheat? Why can't we make it into something at home?"

Since 1986, when she and husband Dave opened the Kansas Wheat House, she does get to keep part of the harvest—400 bushels that she uses to create dozens of unique wheat products, from chicken-fried wheat and baked wheat au gratin to gift baskets with bread mix, "flip 'n flap jacks" (pancake mix), and sunflower suckers.

To satisfy your wheat tooth, stop by the Kansas Wheat House at 102 South Main Street in Cimarron, order a catalog (800-261-6251), or check out the Web site at www.Kansasgrown.com/Kswheat/.

★ ★

Dance All Night to the Dodge City Cow-Boy Band

Dodge City

Matt Dillon may be fictitious, but there really was a Long Branch Saloon, owned at various times by different folks, none of who, unfortunately, was named Miss Kitty.

Between 1878 and 1883, the Long Branch was owned by one Chalk Beeson, who was also the guy who formed the world-famous Dodge City Cow-Boy Band. This brass band, led by a conductor keeping time with a pearl-handled six-shooter, had gigs at Madison Square Garden, the Chicago World's Fair, and Benjamin Harrison's 1889 presidential inauguration.

Band members wore gray cowboy hats, flannel shirts, leather chaps, spurs, and holsters with Colt .45s. Beeson loved to say that despite some folks' claims that the band was made up of musicians and not cowboys, any one of the band members could easily throw a steer over a horse in ten seconds flat.

After their raging success at Harrison's inauguration, the Dodge City Cow-Boy Band launched a two-year world tour. Unfortunately, it only lasted six months. The band had its last hurrah in the Spanish-American War, entertaining the 2nd U.S. Cavalry in Cuba.

To see photos of the notorious band, visit the Boot Hill Museum, which has the old cemetery, Front Street, and a nightly cancan show. It's located on US 400 (also called Wyatt Earp Boulevard) just west of downtown. Phone (620) 227-8188 or visit www.boothill.org.

Down Under

Ellinwood

Ellinwood may be the world's best town for weathering a tornado. Underneath the business district is an underground city that could easily fit the town's entire population and then some.

Back in the 1880s, when the underground city was fully operating, a passenger on the Atchison, Topeka and Santa Fe could get a

★ ★

haircut and a bath and then travel, via the secret underground passageway beneath Main Street, to an underground saloon.

In its heyday, Ellinwood's underground, which ran the full length of the business district, had Jung's Barber Shop, John Weber's Sample Room, Petz Meat Market, Wolitz Shoe Shop, Tom Drake's Harness Shop, a bathhouse, several saloons, and quite possibly an unmentionable place where "ladies of the night" entertained.

Several theories abound as to why the underground city was built back in the late 1800s. The most likely (and this part we know) is that Ellinwood was settled by beer-loving Germans. When changes

Ellinwood's underground city.
PHYLLIS MILLER

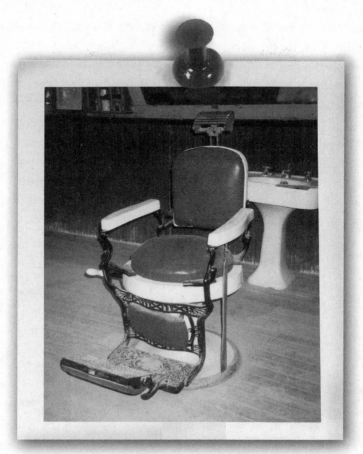

Back when a shave an' a haircut was two bits.
PHYLLIS MILLER

in state liquor laws forced the closing of the town's highly successful aboveground brewery, the settlers probably did what any sensible
beer lover would do. They went underground.

All but three of the underground's eight entrances (you had to lift
wooden sidewalks to gain entry) have been sealed off, and most of
the underground stores have been filled with sand.

Adrianna Dierolf, who rediscovered the underground city in 1980

★ ★

after inheriting her grandfather's building, has managed to preserve
50 feet of tunnel, the harness shop, the barbershop, and the bathhouse. The barbershop still has faded pieces of Victorian wallpaper,
wainscoting of cypress, a beaded ceiling, an old barber's chair, and a
poker table. The bathhouse, with its stone walls and wooden floors,
has graffiti left by a fastidious cowpoke who figured his wages right
on the wall.

Until she sold it in 1992, Dierolf led tours by flashlight. It's still
open for tours, but you have to call and make an appointment. The
old Dick Building, where the tours begin, is located at the northwest
corner of Main and Santa Fe Streets at the stoplight on US 56. Call
Bill Starr at (620) 564-2400.

Dodge City Flicks

Gunsmoke, a popular TV show set in this
notorious cowboy town, ran for twenty
years and 635 episodes before it bit the
trail dust in 1975. But did you know the
TV series was not an original idea? Not only was there a radio show
also called *Gunsmoke*, which aired 413 episodes, but dozens of Dodge
City movies came first. To name just a few:

- *Dodge City Trail*, 1936
- *Dodge City*, 1939, starring Errol Flynn
- *The King of Dodge City*, 1941
- *Vigilantes of Dodge City*, 1944
- *West of Dodge City*, 1947
- *Desperadoes of Dodge City*, 1948
- *Gunfight at Dodge City*, 1958 (before *Gunfight at the OK Corral*)

★ ★

Trivia

It was July 1884. Gunfights had been outlawed, and the rabble-rousing Dodge City was looking for a new adrenaline rush.

A. B. Webster, a former mayor, decided to host America's first official bullfight.

Within twenty-four hours of his brainstorm, Webster had raised $10,000, hired five matadors from Mexico, and corralled a pen of twelve snorting bulls.

Despite warnings from the American Society for the Prevention of Cruelty to Animals, Webster and his Dodge City Driving Park and Fair Association built a grandstand for 4,000 and a 100-foot bullring, and attracted reporters from all over the United States.

Water-ski Kansas
Garden City

The public swimming pool in Garden City is big. Put enough adjectives in front of it and it's the world's largest. But rather than convince you that it's the largest free concrete outdoor municipal pool in the entire known universe, I'd rather tell you that it's big enough for a motorboat with two skiers. The Jaycees used to host bathtub races in it, and the reason the City Council is currently considering closing it down for leaks is because the elephants from the Lee Richardson Zoo (right across the street) used to take baths in it. But here are the facts: The swimming pool holds 2.5 million gallons of water, it takes up half a city block, and its dimensions are 337 feet by 218 feet.

To swim free of charge, visit the pool in Finnup Park (620-276-1255) at 504 East Maple Street, right across from the zoo.

★ ★

Elvis Spotted in Pizza Hut Delivery Box
Garden City

Give Jessie Montes a stack of Pizza Hut boxes and he's likely to find
Elvis Presley. Give him a few refrigerator boxes and he might find
Wyatt Earp, Tiger Woods, Jay Leno, or even Antonio Banderas. Using
tweezers, razor blades, glue, and corrugated cardboard that he cuts
into ¼-inch strips, Montes makes 3-D cardboard-inlay portraits and
3-D sculptures that look like they've been carved from wood. His

Dream Catcher, a 3-D sculpture made from recycled cardboard.

rendition of Frank Sinatra sold for $2,250 at a New York City art gallery, and a more recent sculpture sold for ten grand.

A former janitor for Dodge City High School, Montes had thrown away plenty of boxes before he recognized their potential as an art medium. In 1990, when his daughter was sent to the Gulf War, he needed something to calm his nerves, so he began cutting up boxes and gluing them together. In 1994, he showed a portrait he'd made of William Shakespeare to the high school art teacher.

The teacher was blown away. Her encouragement sparked Montes on.

In 1998, Duane West, a Garden City attorney, saw a show of Montes's unique artwork at the Garden City Community College. Not only did he buy the entire show of twenty-five pieces, he signed on to be his agent.

"This guy's a genius," West says. "He deserves all the recognition I can get him."

Although Jessie's work is available at galleries around the country, the biggest gallery is right in Duane West's Garden City basement. You can view Duane's personal collection (it has grown from twenty-five to thirty-seven, including a 24- by 32-inch portrait of Barack Obama), with another hundred or more for sale. Call (620) 276-6754 to schedule an appointment.

The Great Plague of Grasshopper Postcards
Garden City

In the dust bowl days of the 1930s, Kansas swarmed with grasshoppers. Lots of people packed up and moved west, but Frank "Pop" Conard, a Garden City photographer and owner of a local radio station, decided to make the best of the disaster.

One morning at 3:00, while thinking about the grasshoppers, he came up with the idea of turning them into a joke. Later that day, with the help of his trusty camera, he began making funny montages of people and giant grasshoppers.

★ ★

Calling them "hopper whoppers," he made postcards of grasshoppers holding up trains, grasshoppers fighting men with sticks, and grasshoppers sprawled out on giant flatbed trucks. They sold like wildfire at cabin camps, service stations, and tourist spots.

By the time he retired in 1963, Conard had sold some 3 million hopper whoppers.

Replicas of the postcards are still for sale at the Finney County Historical Museum, 403 South Fourth Street in Garden City, (620) 272-3664.

HOWDY FOLKS HERE I COME.

Yeehaw!!!
FINNEY COUNTY HISTORICAL MUSEUM

Hairballs R Us
Garden City

While calling around to find Pop Conard postcards, I discovered that I'd nearly overlooked another of Garden City's premier tourist attractions.

The Finney County Historical Museum is the proud owner of the world's largest hairball. It was found inside the stomach of a cow at Iowa Beef Processors in nearby Holcomb. When wet, it weighs 55 pounds. It's dry in the display case, so the weight dips to a mere 20 pounds, but even then it measures 37 inches in circumference. I probably don't need to tell you that that's bigger than a basketball.

Hairball today, hairball tomorrow.
FINNEY COUNTY HISTORICAL MUSEUM

Another meat-packing plant recently offered the historical society a second large hairball, but they turned it down. Probably a wise decision. Put two hairballs of that magnitude in one place and crowd control becomes a problem.

Finney County Historical Museum is at 403 South Fourth Street, near the entrance to the zoo. Phone (620) 272-3664.

Rollin', Rollin', Rollin', Keep Those Tumbleweeds Rollin'

Prairie Tumbleweed Farm is living proof that you can sell absolutely anything on the Internet.

Linda Katz was just kidding when she asked her son to put up a family Web site offering tumbleweeds for sale. Calling the site Prairie Tumbleweed Farm, she listed big tumbleweeds at $25, midsize tumbleweeds at $15, and economy-size tumbleweeds at $10. Was she ever surprised that within two months of putting up the site, she'd received more than 2,000 orders, including a $1,000 order from the children's TV show *Barney & Friends*.

Never mind that she didn't have a farm at all (she lived in a subdivision) and had never even so much as touched a tumbleweed. She quickly recruited her five nieces and nephews to gather tumbleweeds—not a difficult task in western Kansas, where they clog drainage ditches, pile up in fencerows, and have even been known to cause traffic accidents.

Tumbleweeds from Katz's "farm" are boxed and shipped to addresses all over the world. Customers include TV and movie producers, home decorators, scientists, and some nutty folks who prefer the Russian thistle bushes over Christmas trees. They're so popular in Japan that Katz now also offers the Web site in Japanese.

To order your very own tumbleweed Christmas tree, check out the company's humorous Web site at www.prairietumble weedfarm.com or call (620) 276-8954.

Within two months of putting up her Prairie Tumbleweed Farm Web site, Linda sold more than 2,000 of the biggest and roundest tumble-weeds Kansas had to offer.
LINDA KATZ PRAIRIE TUMBLEWEED FARM

★ ★

All the Whos Down in Mixville Liked Scrap Metal a Lot
Great Bend

If you've looked everywhere for a Reel Supersonic Espresso-powered Bug Sucker and still come up empty-handed, consider a trip to Great Bend. Bob Mix, a metal fabricator by day and a mad scientist/da Vinci by night, has at least one he could loan you. He also has a pint-size pool shark welded from scrap metal, a 5-foot *Hesperornis regalis* with a spine made from a drilling rig gear chain, and a miniature castle he welded for his wife, Beverly, when it became obvious his promise to

Bob Mix and his talking junk.
STEVE SCHULTZ

✦ ✦

"build her a castle" wasn't coming true as quickly as he'd hoped.

Mix, who works and lives in Mixville, a trailer park near Great Bend where several family members live, can make anything. Tell him what you want, wait while it percolates in his creative mind, and before long he'll have made it out of something he either found or concocted from scrap metal. Mix has made miniature motorcycles, alien fishermen, German war machines, English mastiffs, a family tree out of old car tires, and a Chariot of the Gods cycle that his grandson pedals proudly through Mixville.

Mix's biggest thrill is taking things that nobody else wants and giving them new life.

"Junk talks to me," he says. "I walk by it and it tells me what it wants me to do."

Mix's work can be seen at the Grassroots Art Center at 213 South Main Street in Lucas.

Green, Green, My World is Green
Greensburg

Naming this 1886 town after local stagecoach owner Donald "Cannonball" Green turned out to be an omniscient decision. A hundred and twenty-one years later, Greensburg, after 95 percent of the town was flattened by an EF5 tornado, decided to rebuild as an environmentally friendly, green model town. In essence, city leaders said, "We have a blank slate. Let's do something extraordinary."

Not only did they decide to rebuild all public buildings with LEED platinum standards (it's the Holy Grail of green building, only 125 have been built so far), but they established a nonprofit called "Green Town" that is building twelve demonstration homes, each of which will showcase a different green building technique. The first, a silo-turned-ecohouse that officially opened in 2009, even has a guest suite for overnight lodging.

"It's one thing to read about new, ecologically sound building practices, but it's something else to see how they work," says Daniel

Wallach, founder of Greensburg Green Town, a group that provides outreach and education.

Ecotourists from around the world flock to Greensburg to tour the "living laboratory" with such features as solar electricity, rooftop vegetable gardens, cisterns for water catchment, and dual-flush toilets and to meet Greensburg's many greeniuses (green experts). They've won praise and media attention from everyone from Leonardo DiCaprio, who produced a Discovery Channel series on Greensburg's new green vibe, to CNN and BBC.

Greensburg's Green Town can be reached at 204 West Florida, Greensburg, KS 67504, (620) 723-2790, www.greensburggreentown .org.

Well, Well, Well
Greensburg

I'm happy to report that Greensburg's world largest hand-dug well, long a stand-out tourist attraction, was one of the few things that survived the tornado with flying colors. Unfortunately, the gift shop behind the big well flew off with Dorothy, and for legal reasons, no one has been allowed down the four flights of metal steps since.

Thankfully, the 109-foot well, which was excavated in 1887 with shovels, picks, pulleys, and ropes, is expected to reopen in 2010 when the new gift shop is rebuilt. Needless to say, Greensburg had a few other priorities.

The humongous well was built by the big cheese at Santa Fe Railroad, who were racing the Rock Island Line across the country. They figured a well to power the steam locomotives would give the company a leg up. For more than a year, crews of twelve to fifteen farmers, cowboys, and itinerants were hired each morning at sunup and paid $1 a day to dig.

Despite their hard work, the Rock Island Line won the race, the Santa Fe tracks were dismantled, and the giant well was left to provide the railroad-less town with water. It did a good job for fifty

★ ★

years, but in 1937 the city of Greensburg came up with an alternative water source and the well was turned into a tourist attraction.

Eventually, guests will once again be able to climb the steps into the gigantic man-made hole. The big well is located at 315 South Sycamore Street in Greensburg, or you can call (620) 723-4102 or check them out at www.bigwell.org.

In Cold Blood
Holcomb

Before Charles Manson, Son of Sam, and Jeffrey Dahmer, there were Perry Smith and Richard Hickock, two ex-cons who met in a Lansing prison. On November 14, 1959, they drove to Holcomb and murdered Herbert Clutter, his wife, Bonnie, and two of their four kids.

The crime was all the more shocking considering that Holcomb, a town of fewer than 200 people, was a quiet, unassuming little community that no one would have ever heard of had Truman Capote not spent five years and 343 pages on it in his best-selling true crime novel, *In Cold Blood*. Smith and Hickock got a bad tip from a fellow con who had once worked for Herb Clutter, the prosperous owner of River Valley Farm. Mistakenly believing he left thousands of dollars in the family safe, Smith and Hicock left the scene of the crime with nothing but $50, a transistor radio, and binoculars. They were executed for the four murders in 1965.

Fifty-some years later, the Clutters' murder site, a five-bedroom, two-story brick and clapboard house, still attracts interested folks who drive 8 miles west of Garden City to see it.

What a Gas!
Hugoton

Kansas has a gas field that's five times bigger than the state of Rhode Island. It's the largest gas field in North America.

Millions of years ago, when the earth's crust was rumbling and roaring and pushing up the Rocky Mountains, Kansas got left with

★ ★

an abundance of natural gas and oil. Not a bad geological trade-off when you think about it. Colorado gets Marla Maples in Bogner. We get enough natural gas to heat every home in the state for at least 364 years.

Natural gas, which forms between layers of chalk, shale, limestone, and sandstone, is often accompanied by helium. Sure enough, the Hugoton Gas Field also contains the world's largest reserve of helium.

To learn more about the Hugoton Gas Field, stop by the Stevens County Gas and Historical Museum in Hugoton. It's open 1 to 5 p.m. Monday through Friday and 2 to 4 p.m. Saturday and Sunday at 905 South Adams Street, (620) 544-8751.

Those Carousel Ponies Sure Beat Plow Horses
Kinsley

In 1901, Charles Brodbeck, a farmer from Kinsley, about fell off his horse when he saw a cable-driven carousel in Hutchinson that people were willingly forking over five whole cents to ride. "Why," he mused, "would people ride their real horses to a carousel with wooden horses and pay money to go round and round?"

He thought about it so hard that the next year he went back to the Hutchinson carousel and traded a quarter acre of his own land for the durned thing. For a while, he set it in his pasture, giving rides to neighbors, but in 1908 he and his son loaded the steam-powered carousel onto a flatbed, transported it around the state, and started charging for rides.

It didn't take the Brodbecks long to figure out that there was a lot more money in carnivals than there was in agriculture. They sold a little more of their land and bought a Ferris wheel. Before long, it was their full-time occupation.

Among the various Brodbeck family members, there were six complete carnivals operating out of little Kinsley, which barely has a population of 1,500. Three of the better-known carnival companies in the country had Kinsley addresses.

By the late 1970s, the Kinsley carnival companies were defunct, but in 1998, the National Foundation for Carnival Heritage decided to set up shop in Kinsley. The town now has a wonderful museum with one of only seven remaining Heyn carousels (the other six are owned by a German collector), old games of chance, antique ticket booths, and hand-painted banners. In the adjoining Hall of Fame, you'll see exhibits about Kinsley sword swallowing teams and Her Sexcellency, Sally Rand, a famous carnival dancer.

To spin the 1920 wheel of chance, visit the Carnival Heritage Center at 200 East Sixth Street, (620) 659-2201.

Better Than Colt .45s and Dedicated U.S. Marshals
LaCrosse

For years, nothing could put a crimp in the Wild West's crazy gunslingers and cattle rustlers. But then barbed wire was invented in 1874 and strung across the prairies. Cattle rustlers and cowboys had little choice but to calm down. No wonder its inventor claimed it was "cheaper than dirt and stronger than steel."

LaCrosse, which holds the title of Barbed Wire Capital of the World, has a museum dedicated to the formidable fencing, and hosts an annual Swap and Sell, where barbed wire collectors from around the country converge. The museum features some 2,100 types and styles of devil's rope (that's what they called it back then), a seventy-two-pound crow's nest made of barbed wire, and a collection of barbed wire liniments, potions that were sold to cure cuts and injuries incurred by man or beast.

At the Swap and Sell, held the first weekend in May, there's a riveting splicing contest in which splicers armed with nothing but leather gloves are required to put a barbed wire fence back together, strong enough to suspend a seventy-five-pound weight.

The Museum of Barbed Wire is located at 120 West First Street and can be contacted at (785) 222-9900 or www.rushcounty.org/BarbedWireMuseum/.

★ ★

Diplomatic Relations in Pancake Flipping
Liberal

In 1949, R. J. Leete, president of the Liberal Jaycees, heard about a unique pancake-flipping race in Olney, England. He wrote to the vicar of Olney's St. Peter's and Paul's Church, the sponsor of the centuries-old race, and challenged him to an international match. The housewives of Liberal, he proposed, would race against the housewives of Olney.

Olney, of course, had a leg up. They'd been flipping pancakes and racing with skillets since 1445, when one of the church members got so caught up in her pancake making that she almost missed the Shrove Tuesday church service. Because lard was forbidden during Lent, the women of the village fried stacks and stacks of pancakes in order to use up their remaining fat stashes. Still clad in her apron, with a skillet in her hand, the tardy woman raced to church flipping the last of her pancakes as she ran. The next year, her neighbors decided to get in on the act, challenging her to a race with skillets, aprons, and pancakes. Running from the town pump to the church steps every year, the winner of the race is presented with a "kiss of peace" by the bell ringer.

The Olney vicar liked Leete's suggestion, and on February 21, 1950, the first International Pancake Race was staged. It has been held every year since, attracting thousands of visitors and loads of media attention. So much, in fact, that the 1980 race was declared a tie because a television news truck inadvertently blocked the finish line in Olney.

To watch the Liberal race, which runs from Sixth and Kansas Streets to Third and Lincoln Streets, be on hand about quarter till noon any Shrove Tuesday. To get a copy of the pancake recipe (it serves 100 and uses 280 pounds of pancake mix, 10 dozen eggs, and 35 gallons of water), check out www.pancakeday.net or call (620) 620-6423.

★ ★

There's No Place Like Dorothy's House
Liberal

What do Salman Rushdie, Carl Sagan, and Gloria Estefan have in common? At one time or another, all of them were members of I.W.O.C. Never heard of it? It's the International Wizard of Oz Club, and the above-mentioned are just three of the club's 3,000 members. Founded in 1957, the club tracks all things having to do with L. Frank Baum and *The Wizard of Oz,* which means they're certainly up on Liberal, Kansas. Not only does Liberal have Dorothy's house—a 1907 farmhouse that looks just like the house she couldn't wait to return to—they also have a 5,000-square-foot animated *Wizard of Oz* complex and twenty Dorothy tour guides, all of whom went through an intensive two-week Dorothy training.

That's right, if you fork over the $5 admission fee, you'll be led by one of the Dorothys (of course she'll be wearing a blue-checked gingham dress and red ruby slippers) down the yellow brick road. You'll see animated Munchkins, good and bad witches, talking trees, and winged monkeys. At the end of the tour, if you can still stand more, you can hurry to the gift shop in the Coronado Museum (it's on the same grounds), where the movie is shown from the moment the museum opens until it closes.

Every second weekend in October, the museum hosts a two-day Oz Fest. Visit the museum at 567 Yellow Brick Road (aka Cedar) or call (620) 624-7624 or go to www.dorothyshouse.com.

Birth of a (Hatchet-wielding) Nation
Medicine Lodge

If only Al-Anon had existed back in 1899, Carry A. Nation, the infamous hatchet-wielding teetotaler from Medicine Lodge, Kansas, could have saved herself a lot of jail time.

Until that fateful day in 1899 when Carry and Mrs. Wesley Cain, fellow chairman of the Medicine Lodge Women's Christian

★ ★

Temperance Union, put on their best dresses and bonnets and headed to Mort Strong's Saloon, Nation lived a relatively quiet life.

She was a preacher's wife, a mom, and a devout Christian, thanks to six years of a youthful illness that required bed rest and study of the Bible. Sure, she fought with her second husband, David Nation, tried to write his sermons and coach him on proper elocution, but overall, she was just an everyday common citizen.

But once the fervor of the temperance movement began boiling in her veins, there was no stopping her. Not only did she successfully close down all seven saloons in Medicine Lodge, she went on a national rampage, chopping up saloons with rocks, clubs, and hatchets. Eventually, her infamy prompted speaking engagements at Carnegie Hall, lecture tours of Europe (where she tried to convince England of the evils of tea), and a nationally distributed newsletter called *The Smasher's Mail.*

As for the Al-Anon . . . Carry's hatred of demon rum had less to do with Kansas being the first state to make liquor illegal and more to do with her first husband, Dr. Charles Gloyd, who drank himself to death before Carry was twenty-four, leaving her with an infant daughter.

To buy a miniature hatchet, a silver or gold version of the one Carry often sold to raise jail bond, visit the brick home that Carry and her second husband, David Nation, bought for $2,500 in 1880 when they moved to Kansas from Texas. On the National Register of Historic Places, the home is now a museum at 209-211 West Fowler Street, (620) 886-3553.

Crossed Smoke Signals
Medicine Lodge

In 1867, before Carry Nation came along, Medicine Lodge hosted Dog Fat, Iron Mountain, Black Kettle, Ten Bears, Kicking Eagle, Gap in the Wood, Standing Feather, and 15,000 other Kiowa, Comanche, Cheyenne, Arapaho, and Apache Indians who made the mistake of

believing government commissioners who promised to quit killing
buffalo in return for the right to build railroads across their lands.

The Medicine Lodge Peace Treaty, a historic treaty that basically
marked the beginning of the end for native ways, was signed October 21, 1867, on the banks of the Medicine River and Elm Creek.
The 15,000 Indians from the five Great Plains tribes set up camp near
this sacred native spot, and 500 cavalry soldiers, federal bigwigs, and
reporters from around the world showed up.

In case you're wondering the outcome of the treaty, just look
around. The trains, of course, zoom by at the rate of hundreds a day.
The buffalo? Let's just say the herds that once covered the plains are
long gone.

Every three years, the city of Medicine Lodge reenacts the famous
peace treaty. It's no small feat. The show alone employs 1,200 actors.
Thousands show up at the native rock amphitheater for the three-day
celebration, which has been going on since 1927. For more info, call the
Peace Treaty Office, at (620) 886-9815, or visit www.peacetreaty.org.

Claude, Claude, Claude of the Jungle
Montezuma

Ever been to Angkor, Cambodia, or Trondheim, Norway? Claude
Stauth and his wife, Donnie, sure have. In fact, the longtime residents
of Montezuma (population 879) traveled to ninety-five countries
on six continents before they died and left their entire collection of
"travel souvenirs" to their "family," the citizens of Montezuma.

Their extensive collection of rare indigenous art, tribal instruments,
weapons, costumes, and statues is housed in a striking earth-colored
copper-roofed structure worthy of any large city.

In addition to berber daggers, thumb pianos from Cameroon,
and carved lion leg bones, the Stauth Memorial Museum showcases
bookends, lamps, and ashtrays made from parts of big game animals.

They're not from countries you can't pronounce. They were made
right here in Kansas by Ralph Fry, a hunter and the Stauths' neighbor,

who owned a hardware store in town but was so avid in his conservation practices that he was made an honorary game warden. The weird lamps and bookends were the result of Fry's belief in using all parts of the animals he shot. There are also lots of big moose heads and exotic game animals in the Fry collection.

The Stauths, generous folks that they were, wanted the museum to go beyond their personal travels, so a large portion of the museum is dedicated to traveling exhibits from such sources as the Smithsonian Institution and the London Museum of Natural History. Donnie also designated one room of the building for her bridge club.

To see lip disks from Bunia, carved lion leg bones from Goma, and ivory from Nepal, visit the Stauth Memorial Museum at 111 North Aztec Street in Montezuma, (620) 846-2527, (www.stauthmemorial museum.org).

Political Cartoons on Highway 400
Mullinville

M. T. Liggett would never call himself an artist. He had enough of that in grade school, when his art teacher told the class to paint a dinosaur, then frowned on the fact that Liggett painted his purple and gave it wings.

No, he had a good career in the Air Force, didn't take up art—or what some people like to think of as art—until he retired to the family farm in Mullinville. With tousled silver hair, a red bandanna, overalls, and black cowboy hat, Liggett could easily pass for a typical Kansas farmer.

Until you see his totems—wild political statements mounted on poles, standing side by side, many moving in the wind. Working from an old house he painted and calls the "wacky shack," Liggett has been taking the junk farmers leave down by the barn and welding it into his controversial interpretations of the world.

Hundreds of totems lampooning everything from Monica Lewinsky's blue dress and Roller Derby queens to what Liggett calls

Political lampoonery at its best.
STEVE SCHULTZ

★ ★

Trivia

Just outside Montezuma is 20 square miles of windmills. Gray County Wind Energy, owner of the windmill farm, erected 170 windmills, each of which weighs 147,000 pounds and generates massive BPUs of electricity.

"Doctor Lorena Bobbitt" and Archimedes line a ½-mile stretch on US 400.

For a while, the powers that be tried to outlaw them, tried to impose a roadside ban, said they caused too much of a disturbance. Luckily, the ban didn't stick, and Liggett continues to caricature politicians and their bureaucratic nonsense.

To view Liggett's political lampoonery, drive west on US 400 from Mullinville. You can't miss them.

Spiker and the Gang
Scott City

To say the Keystone Gallery is in Scott City is a bit misleading. This unique art gallery/curio shop/fossil hunting headquarters is actually in the middle of the Kansas Niobrara chalk formation, 18 miles north of Scott City. A herd of 200 buffalo roam nearby. The closest structure over two stories is Monument Rocks. But since Scott City is where Chuck Bonner and his wife, Barbara Shelton, get their mail, that's where they claim to be from. Their gallery has at least two distinctions separating it from other art gallery/curio shop/fossil hunting headquarters. First, the limestone building used to be a Pilgrim Holiness Church, built in 1916 by locals hankering for a little religion. Second, it meets all its electricity needs from the sun and the wind.

★ ★

When Bonner and Shelton decided to renovate the little church in 1981, they figured the last thing they needed to do was depend on the mainstream electric grid. They went in with shovels, cleared out the debris (the church had been abandoned since 1950), and added solar panels and a wind charger.

Show up at the gallery and you never know what Bonner, a painter and fossil hunter, might be up to. He could be leading fossil hunters on an expedition to the Smoky Hill River Valley in Spiker, his 1949 Chevy Suburban, or he could be painting in the back room. If he's around, he's happy to tell you everything he knows about the museum's (yes, it's a museum, too) late-Cretaceous study collection. Bonner and Shelton themselves have found one hundred significant fossils, many of which now reside at universities and natural history museums around the country. They're particularly proud of a 4-foot

Mugging for the camera!
KEYSTONE GALLERY

★ ★

Trivia

Plains has the widest main street in America. Grand Avenue, the main drag through this tiny town in Meade County, measures 155 feet and 5 inches across, inspiring Ripley's Believe It or Not! to give it the record-breaking nod. All we know is it takes sixty-nine hand-holding fourth graders to reach storefront to storefront, and if you want to holler at your neighbor across the street, you better take a megaphone.

skull of a Pterandodon, a flying reptile, that's on display at the Natural History Museum of Los Angeles County.

To see Bonner's unique collection or buy everything from black-and-white mosasaur T-shirts to Onyx fiber-optic spheres, visit the Keystone Gallery, 18 miles north of Scott City on US 83 (620-872-2762; www.keystonegallery.com).

That's One Way to Beat the Tax Man
Ulysses

During western migration, towns all over newly settled lands fought rigorous battles over who would get the county seat, who would get the railroad. Ulysses, which did outwit Appomattox in the struggle for Grant County seat, ended up going so far into debt to do it that the whole town was in danger of foreclosure.

A few months before government tax men came to foreclose, however, a contingent of folks led by George Washington Earp (Wyatt's cousin and the mayor of the town) loaded the town's twelve restaurants, four hotels, and twelve saloons onto rollers and moved them 3 miles west. When the foreclosure agents showed up, the only thing left was a masonry school.

You can hear all about the town that outwitted the tax man at the Historic Adobe Museum and Hotel Edwards, a restored frontier hotel, located at 300 East Oklahoma Street (620-356-3009; www.historicadobemuseum.org).

Shoo, Fly, Don't Bother Me

The flyswatter was invented in Kansas. It all started with the *Mosquito Gazette*, a weekly newsletter published in 1906 by Dr. Samuel Crumbine, the state's first secretary of health. Believing that flies were the main source of typhoid fever, Crumbine headlined a summer issue of his state medical bulletin with the words "Swat the Fly."

Frank Rose, a Weir City teacher and local Boy Scout leader, saw that issue of the *Gazette* and wanted his troop to be involved. He bought wire mesh, which his scouts cut into squares and attached to wooden yardsticks given away by the local drugstore.

Crumbine, who often dressed in a Prince Albert coat with a six-shooter strapped to his hip, was also partially responsible for the invention of Dixie cups. One of his first goals as executive secretary of the brand-new state board of health was to outlaw public drinking cups. Hugh Moore, an ex-Kansan living in New England, showed Crumbine samples of a throwaway cup he'd made from paper. Crumbine suggested he sell his invention in penny vending machines on railroad cars. This cup was the first product Moore manufactured in his new business, the Dixie Cup Company.

index

index

index

index

index

★ ★

index

index

index

index

index